Crime and Punishment in Victorian Edinburgh

Crime and Punishment in Victorian Edinburgh

Lynne Wilson

Crime and Punishment in Victorian Edinburgh

Lynne Wilson

Copyright © Lynne Wilson, 2016

Published by Honeyman & Wilson

Also by Lynne Wilson

A Year in Victorian Edinburgh (Kindle and Paperback)

Deadly Victorian Remedies (eBook and Paperback)

Contents

Introduction	*Page 1*
Chapter One – Police Court	*Page 7*
Chapter Two – Sheriff Court	*Page 34*
Chapter Three – High Court	*Page 60*
Chapter Four – Notorious Cases and Executions	*Page 78*
Chapter Five – Forensic Medicine and the Victorian Expert Witness	*Page 100*
Chapter Six – Prison	*Page 109*
Acknowledgements	*Page 117*
Bibliography	*Page 118*
Glossary	*Page 120*
Victorian Money Conversion Guide	*Page 122*

Introduction

The 19th century saw many changes in the way crime was dealt with in Scotland. Scottish burghs were given power in 1833 to establish police forces if they had not already done so. Edinburgh however, due to the passing of the Edinburgh Police Act in 1805, already had a dedicated, uniformed police force to patrol the city.

Princes Street, Edinburgh © Peter Stubbs, Edinphoto

The remit of the police at this time extended to maintaining sanitary conditions, and police duties included: 'Watching, Lighting, Cleansing, Regulation of the Keeping of Pigs, Asses, Dogs, and other inferior animals; Regulation of the lodging houses for the poorer classes; and preventing the undue accumulation of filth or manure'. Additionally, the job of police constable was not a well paid position and with the long working hours, the police force in the early part of Victoria's reign often consisted of recruits who were less than suitable and it was not uncommon to see constables appearing in court for crimes they themselves had committed. However, gradual improvements were made and a report by Her Majesty's Inspector of Constabulary for Scotland in 1898, highlighted the 'greater efficiency and more general usefulness' that had been attained in the force in recent years. This had been achieved it seems, by a number of factors, such as: improving the pay and implementing pay rises after approved periods of service; supplying better and more suitable uniforms; providing suitable police stations, offices, and cells; mounting officers on bicycles; the extension of 'telephonic communication' in police jurisdictions; providing the new 'Police Manual'; providing 'ambulance instruction' and the introduction of a complete ambulance kit at the principal stations; instruction in baton and physical drill; and the provision of noiseless boots for night duty. The report also emphasised the importance of the detective branch of the service, in order to have trained and qualified officers specifically retained for criminal work, and who could continue investigations without taking officers away from their beats.

The emergence of these 'Detective Officers' during Victoria's reign greatly assisted in the efforts against criminality, with detectives such as James McLevy, a well known figure at this time, using the knowledge of local offenders and rapport they had built up to get to bottom of cases. McLevy often wrote about the cases he worked on and these stories were later published.

The emergence of a democracy, combined with an increase in the number of statutes also led to significant reforms in the law, with Legal writers such as George Joseph Bell, Professor of Scots Law at Edinburgh (1822-1843), introducing texts on the principles of the law in Scotland. In the later part of the 19th Century, Criminal Procedure was reviewed by the

Criminal Procedure Act 1887. Around this time judges also produced standard texts to deal with disputes such as: Wills and Succession; Husband and Wife; Parent and Child; and Master and Servant. Employment Law was also developed during this time with the introduction of The Trade Union Act 1871, the Employers and Workmen Act 1875 and the Workmen's Compensation Act 1897.

The Edinburgh courts, like all courts in Scotland, dealt separately with Summary offences and Indictable offences. Summary offences were dealt with either by the Police (or Burgh) Court or the Sheriff Court. These ranged from the more petty offences to assaults. Indictable offences were dealt with by the Sheriff and Jury Court or the High Court of Justiciary. These were typically serious assaults, fraud or murder. It was not unusual at this time to receive a fairly lengthy prison sentence for crimes which we would probably describe as 'petty' today, such as in the case of the 'Sweetie Vendor' named Butters, who ended up in prison for selling sweets to children on a Sunday. However, on the other hand, it was also common for some violent crimes to attract a lenient sentence. Women could often receive a greater sentence than men for the same crimes, as committing crime went against the Victorian image of 'womanliness'. A letter to the editor of the Scotsman in 1857 from an Edinburgh resident highlights this disparity:

'Considering that justice should be even handed and punishment commensurate with crime, I beg to call attention to the following cases which appeared on the very same page of your paper – "Theft by a Policeman – Yesterday, at the Police Court, Robert Whitehead, a person lately employed in the police force, was found guilty of stealing a watch from a man while the latter was in a state of intoxication in the street. He

was sentenced to sixty days imprisonment with hard labour". The other case to which I have referred is as follows – "Margaret Henry, accused of picking a man's pocket of a purse and money, was sentenced to fifteen months imprisonment". I cannot perceive that a female committing a robbery on a man is worse that the same offence committed by a man; on the contrary, I conceive that the crime having been committed by a policeman was an aggravation.'

In a letter to the editor of the Scotsman in 1891, another Edinburgh resident writes:

'*I wanted to point out the great disparity in the punishments inflicted for assaults and thefts, a state of matters perfectly apparent to any one who reads the daily papers, or who cares to visit the Courts while trials are in progress. It seems to me, and no doubt to a great many other people, that brutal assault is a much more serious crime than paltry theft, and therefore deserving of the heavier penalty*'.

Inside a Victorian Prison

Some crimes of the more 'nuisance' variety would be dealt with by a fine. Offences such as having dirty closes or smoky chimneys are examples of these, along with the crime of beating carpets to remove the dust from them out with the permitted hours. 'Riding Furiously', which was the Victorian equivalent of speeding, was also a crime often seen in the courts.

A report published early in Victoria's reign on 'The State of Crime in Midlothian' attempted to give reasons for the amount of crime in the county, noting that:

'Most of the petty thefts seem to be committed by boys from about eight to eighteen years old. The other offences are by people of various ages and of both sexes. As a class; the offenders are distinguished for habits of drunkenness; many of them have no regular occupation; their education appears to have been generally neglected, and the parents of most of them (well known) are observed to be of bad characters themselves.'

A lack of proper treatment and understanding of mental illness, often resulted in some unfortunate characters ending up in the justice system, such as in the case below in 1874:

Forty year old James Johnstone, described as 'powerfully built' and 'a madman', was arrested on this date after boarding a passenger steamer at Leith and refusing to produce a ticket for the journey. The sergeant of police on duty was called a struggle ensued which started on the ship and continued on the quay, with six men being required to bring Johnstone under control. He was taken to the police office in a wheelbarrow and it was established that he had previously escaped from an asylum.

This book examines the types of crimes each court would have dealt with, including some of the more notorious cases and executions that took place in Edinburgh during the Victorian era, and the emergence of expert witnesses and forensic medicine in criminal cases.

Chapter 1

Police Courts

Police Court Cases in Victorian Edinburgh

29th September 1837

A young girl, described as being 'of tattered and dirty appearance' appeared in the Police Court, charged with taking a petticoat from a five year old child on Calton Hill. She was sentenced to sixty days in the Bridewell.

28th April 1838

Teacher of elocution, John Cameron was called to the bar of the Police Court on 27th April 1838, charged with creating a disturbance at the theatre on the previous night. Cameron, a middle aged man described as 'well shaped and tall, but whose show of manners and outward garb rather belied each other', explained that he had travelled some distance to see the show, paid his shilling for a gallery seat and at the end of the third act he had gone outside for a moment, however on returning he was refused re-admittance. The theatre constable however, gave evidence that Cameron had been kept out because he was very drunk. The magistrate fined him five shillings.

7th October 1838

An 'old offender' was placed at the bar of the Police Court charged with attempting to break into a victualling store at an early hour in the morning. He had made his way halfway down the chimney with a rope fastened round his waist, when he became stuck. The watchman on duty, hearing his cries, rescued the thief then promptly took him to the police office.

13th March 1839

Thomas McEwen, a Market Trader in the Cowgate was convicted in the Police Court for selling 'unwholesome hams'. McEwen had been attempting to sell a quantity of bacon hams, which were said to be 'neither fit for the use of man nor beast'. He was fined two guineas and the hams were ordered to be buried.

23rd June 1841

Thomas Weir, from the West Port, was charged with various acts of swindling, by 'obtaining money from respectable individuals' under false pretences and using false names. Weir's method was to take the family name of those he had practiced upon; and found on his person were several address cards bearing the names of other people.

5th January 1842

Amongst the cases which were the result of what was described as 'the New Year's morning debauches', were two men who had assaulted a night watchman whilst he was doing his rounds. In an assault described as 'wanton and cruel', the night watchman was trampled upon and his clothes were almost torn from his body. The magistrate however, took into account that this was a first offence and fined the men one guinea each.

12th January 1843

Fraud and fortune telling led to a woman named Tillingham being brought before the Police Court on a charge of theft and wilful imposition. Tillingham and another woman were selling small wares and called at a house in Queen Street, where they informed the servants that they were skilled in fortune telling and would disclose some future events to them which were supposedly of the utmost importance and related to their future husbands. One of the girls, duped by this, gave Tillingham some clothing of hers to be taken away and returned later that day with along with her fortune. Needless to say, the fortune teller never returned and the servant girl's clothes were sold on to another person. Tillingham, who was later apprehended in a lodging house in the West Port, was sentenced to twenty days imprisonment.

7th May 1843

In the Police Court on this date were two coal carters who had been observed removing some large pieces of coal from a cart they were driving and placing them behind a wooden shed in Drummond Place. The witness who had seen this informed the police, who ascertained that the two men had been sent from a coal depot in Leith Walk to deliver a cart of coals to a family in Drummond Place, having previously gotten the coals weighed and been given a certificate of weight. On weighing the coals again the police found them to be underweight, due to some of them having been removed on route and hidden in the shed. One of the men, being 'an old offender' was sentenced to sixty days imprisonment and the other was sentenced to thirty days.

17th April 1844

William Hughes, a police constable was placed at the bar in the Police Court charged with being drunk and assaulting John Inglis and Neil Gunn, also officers of the police, whilst they were in the execution of their duty in the Grassmarket on a previous evening. Evidence was given which found the charge proved and the magistrate commented that he was determined to punish every instance of improper police conduct brought before him, and ordered that Hughes be dismissed from the police.

18th December 1844

Two young men described as 'respectable looking' were placed at the Police Court bar charged with a breach of the peace. The charge stated that whilst in Princes Street in the early hours of the morning they behaved 'in an outrageous manner and did riot and fight, whereby a crowd was collected, and a breach of the peace was committed'. Several witnesses for the defence were called, all giving contradictory evidence and as a result the magistrate found the two guilty. Commenting that the case was aggravated by the fact of that it took place on the Sabbath, he fined them ten shillings each or the alternative of ten days in prison.

21st December 1846

Thomas White, described as 'an old offender', appeared at the City Police Court on a charge of stealing from a house in Candleriggs, the second volume of 'Tales of a Grandfather' by Sir Walter Scott. White pleaded guilty and was sentenced to nine months imprisonment.

23rd April 1847

On this date, a case involving four disgruntled former employees of Messrs. Blackwood & Sons, printers and publishers was heard. Unhappy that they had been replaced by staff from England, the four were alleged to have entered the shop, behaved in a 'riotous and disorderly manner' and assaulted the staff present. All received fines ranging from £1 to £6.

15th September 1848

'Keeping Irregular Houses' led to Alexander Purvis being brought before the Police Court on a charge of allowing 'riotous or disorderly conduct within the house occupied by him in Strichen's Close; and also of having knowingly harboured thieves, prostitutes, and disorderly persons'. Purvis, on being found guilty, was sentenced to sixty days imprisonment.

11th January 1849

In the Police Court on this date, two juvenile thieves were sentenced to twenty lashes each, to be inflicted by one of the constables, in sight of the police surgeon. This was a practice which was allowed under the New Police Act, in an attempt to keep young persons out of prison. The thinking was that corporal punishment such as this type of flagellation would give the offender a short, sharp shock and teach them a lesson without their future prospects being compromised by having a prison record.

23rd March 1850

In the few days prior to this date, some twenty or thirty persons had appeared before the magistrate due to street annoyances such as ashes being scattered on the streets in the New Town by persons thought to be 'area sneaks'. Many had been allowed to go away with a caution, with the magistrate advising that servants should be discouraged from employing these 'sneaks' to perform duties which they ought to perform themselves.

27th October 1851

Three girls aged between twelve and eighteen, were brought before the magistrate charged with five or six acts of picking ladies' pockets. The girls, who were described as 'well dressed girls', had been entering shops at busy moments, and while making slight purchases for themselves, taking the opportunity to steal the customers' purses. The girls, after a long and diligent search, were apprehended by criminal officers McLevy and Shaw. The case was remitted to a higher court.

21st June 1852

Two Edinburgh University medical students, Alexander Mackay and Lancelot Armstrong were charged in the Police Court with 'riotous and disorderly conduct in the College Quadrangle'. Mackay was additionally charged with assaulting one of the Masonic procession and Armstrong with assaulting the police and obstructing them in the execution of their duty. Both students pleaded not guilty and the case went to trial. Many witnesses were called for both the prosecution and the defence, with the prosecution witnesses reporting to have seen Mackay strike one of the Freemasons and Armstrong trying to rescue him when he was apprehended. Evidence was also given that Mackay had knocked off one of the masons' hats and that Armstrong had attempted to shut the gates to prevent the cavalry coming in to assist in quashing the disturbance.

Witnesses for the defence gave evidence which contradicted this, however they were found guilty and fined one guinea each.

16th September 1856

Seven young men, described as 'moving in a respectable sphere of society' were charged with disorderly conduct and assault, under very aggravated circumstances. Having been drinking in one of the West Register Street hotels the previous Saturday night, the group, being in a highly intoxicated state on leaving the premises, began indiscriminately attacking passers by, resulting in a scene which was described as a 'disgraceful riot', in which several people, including police officers were injured. It would appear that the seven young gentlemen, who were expecting to receive fines for their behaviour, were 'considerably astonished' when sentences of thirty days imprisonment were given to them.

13th July 1857

Rodger Owen, who was employed by Messrs. Grant & Co., Druggists, appeared at the Police Court on a charge of poisoning of a four year old girl. The girl's mother, Mrs Hay, had attended the Druggists shop on the previous Friday to obtain a mixture for her daughter, who was feeling ill. The mixture, containing calomel, rhubarb and sugar of anise, was prepared by Owen. However after returning home and administering the mixture to her daughter, Mrs Hay began to notice the child becoming very sleepy and early the next morning she was dead. On hearing what had happened, Mr Grant, the owner of the shop looked at the shelf where the calomel bottle was stored, and noticed that the morphia bottle was stored right beside it. Owen later admitted that it was possible that he had mistaken one bottle for the other when he prepared the mixture. The case was remitted to a higher court.

Inside a typical Chemist and Druggist Shop. From the author's own collection.

23rd September 1858

Roman Catholic Priest, William Mackay, found himself in the Police Court after being accused of 'furiously and recklessly driving along the South and North Bridge and assaulting passers by with his riding whip'. The priest admitted that he had carried out these acts and stated that he had lost his temper when some passers by had grabbed hold of his horse, which was a young horse, and not used to being driven through the crowded streets. After expressing his great regret and having been given a severe lecture by the Magistrate, Father Mackay was fined £5.

22nd January 1859

Allowing persons to smoke on the omnibus, lead to conductor Andrew Crighton appearing in the Police Court. Crighton refused to pay a fine of two shillings and sixpence and was therefore sentenced to two days imprisonment.

An Omnibus with passengers. From the author's own collection.

5th September 1859

James Morris and Robert Johnston were charged on this date with a contravention of the Public Houses Act, in selling spirits without a certificate. Morris gave the defence that his house was a club, and the parties who had been supplied with spirits were members of that club.

Johnston's defence was that he was the waiter. On hearing all the evidence, the court decided that there was no proof of their being a club in Morris' house and fined him £3, 10s. Johnston was fined £1, 15s.

23rd February 1860

In the Police Court on this date, the case of the 'Snowball Riot' of Edinburgh came to it's conclusion after a nine day trial. This case seemed to involve fourteen students, who on the date of the incident, had come into conflict with the police in the form of a snowball fight. The disturbance seems to have descended into a riot, due to what many witnesses describe as 'rough usage' by the police, who were reported to have been using their batons vigorously. For the throwing of snowballs, one student was fined £5, twelve other students were each fined £1 and the fourteenth student was admonished.

19th March 1860

Cab driver, William Barclay from Potterow appeared at the Police Court, on a charge of assaulting his wife with a poker. The incident was said to have occurred within their house, and it was alleged that Mrs Barclay had later died as a result of her injuries. The case was remitted to a higher court.

25th April 1860

Robert Swan and Jessie Neil were charged with 'behaving in a riotously and disorderly manner' in the house of the Rev. Mr Davidson in Edinburgh. It appeared that the two accused were accompanying two friends of theirs who wished to get married. They called upon several of the Established clergy of the city, but could find none of them at home. Having adjourned to a tavern in Fleshmarket Close to discuss their options, they were advised by the landlady to try the Rev. Mr Davidson, which they did, but in their excitement at finding him at home, they were unable to convince him that they had the required seriousness for marriage, so he refused to comply with their wishes. After much argument, mostly caused by Swan and Neil, Swan seized Mr Davidson by the collar and swore that he would make him marry his friends. The police were sent for and the whole party were taken to the police office. The bride and bridegroom were allowed to go, as they had been fairly quiet throughout the incident, with Swan and Neil being fined £1 each.

26th August 1865

A quarrel between two men, described as 'frequenters of infamous houses in the High Street' led to one of the men, Mungo Syme, being charged with murder. He and James Kelly had been drinking together in a house in Hyndford's Close, when an argument started between them which developed into a fight. Syme was accused of hitting Kelly several times in the face and knocking him to the ground, resulting in his death. The case was remitted to a higher court.

2nd June 1869

James Little or Jamieson appeared in the Police Court on a charge of breaking a window of a Shoemaker's shop, in an act of revenge against the shop owner. Jamieson, a former soldier, had taken up a life of petty thieving after his discharge. This had led to various short periods in prison, however on the occasion when he stole some boots from Mr Davie's shop, he was given the much lengthier sentence of six years. It appears that on his release from this sentence, he immediately sought out Mr Davie's shop and having procured a stone, threw it at Mr Davie, whom it missed, but broke the window of the shop. Jamieson was sentenced to a further 30 days imprisonment.

10th June 1870

John Safford Fiske appeared in the Police Court on this date, having been apprehended by the Edinburgh police on behalf of the Metropolitan police, who had a warrant for his arrest. The warrant was for what was described as the 'serious charge' of impersonating a woman. Fiske was formally remanded and Superintendent Thomson of the Metropolitan police arrived later that day to escort him back to London on the six o'clock train.

23rd November 1870

One this date, four of the students accused in taking part in the 'Surgeon's Hall Riot' were in the Police Court. This riot had occurred a week previously, when a group of male medical students gathered outside where the newly admitted female medical students were taking an exam, and on their emergence from the building, shouted abuse and threw items at the young women. Female medical students had been seeking admittance to study medicine for some time in Edinburgh, and in October 1869 permission was finally granted for them to begin their studies. However this decision did not meet with everyone's approval and some of the male students and teaching staff endeavoured to make life difficult for the women. After the appalling incident of the 'Surgeon's Hall Riot', some of the more gallant male students at the University made themselves available after their classes to escort the women safely home. Three out of the four students involved in the riot pleaded guilty to breaches of the peace and were each fined £1. The other student, Walter Robertson, pleased not guilty to breach of the peace and an assault on a policeman, but was found guilty by the court and fined £5.

Surgeon's Hall © Peter Stubbs, Edinphoto

3rd December 1870

Neglecting to maintain his wife and children resulted in sixty days imprisonment with hard labour for George Sandilands, a Carter.

11th July 1873

James Macrae, a Bill Poster was charged on this date with 'wilfully and maliciously' covering up part of a space on a board at Haddington Place, Leith with a poster. Macrae, who stated that he had obtained permission from the proprietor of the building to use this space, was fined £3.

26th August 1873

An Irish shoemaker and his family, consisting of wife, daughter, son in law and three sons, were accused of creating a disturbance in their house in the Cannongate early on Sunday morning. One of the accused, on being asked the usual question, 'guilty or not guilty', replied "Yes, your honour, we are all guilty, but we made no noise".

15th September 1873

John Reynolds, a 17 year old described as 'a lad of stunted appearance' was brought up on the charge of creating a disturbance in the Cannongate on Friday. The father of the man, described as 'a decent looking man', pleaded that the case might be dealt with leniently, as the boy had been well behaved until a short time ago, when he had fallen in with bad company. Evidence was given that although Reynolds was a young looking boy, he had become a habitual drunkard, and it was decided that he must be treated by the court as a man. He was therefore sentenced to thirty days imprisonment.

1st July 1874

A man named John Williamson was brought before the Police Court on this date, having been found the previous day indecently dressed. It was stated that Williamson had been 'perambulating the streets destitute of all clothing save a shirt', and appeared in court on this day wrapped in a bed rug. Williamson said that he had come to the city on a visit from Glasgow and he was unable to account for the disappearance of his clothing. He was fined 10s, with the alternative of ten days in prison.

31st August 1874

Cash Clerk, Alex Bonthorn was charged with embezzling approximately £400. The case was postponed until further examination of the books could take place. Bonthorn did not appear in the court, but instead remained at a side door leading from the court to the police cells, apparently suffering from delirium tremens.

5th September 1874

A man named Robert Pate, described by the medical officer as 'a dangerous lunatic', appeared in the police court, accused of having dealt the Rev. George Divorty a blow upon the head with a walking stick. It was ordered that Pate be placed in an asylum.

11th October 1874

A woman named McDonald was sent to prison for sixty days for 'husband beating'. McDonald had thrown a plate at her husband, knocked him down and gave him what was described as 'a severe beating'.

22nd February 1875

James Aitken was brought before the Police Court after being caught in the act of picking a lady's pocket at the booking office of Waverley Station. The Magistrate after considering remitting him to a higher court, decided to sentence him instead to sixty days imprisonment with hard labour.

10th March 1875

At the Police Court on this date, three English football players found themselves charged with causing a disturbance at the Waverley Station.

The accused had been taking part in the International Football Match, and it was alleged that they had assaulted an engine driver and policeman whilst within the railway station. The case was delayed for a week for further evidence to be brought forward.

16th March 1875

David McGibbon, the owner of a 'ferocious and vicious dog' was charged with allowing the dog to be at large in the High Street, the consequence of which was that a boy was bitten on the arm. McGibbon was fined £5 and told that the dog would be destroyed if it was permitted to run about again.

23rd March 1875

A serious charge was made against a man named Thomas Anderson on this date, that in a 'fit of passion' he had seized the ten year old son of his landlord and put him on the fire. Anderson denied the charge, stating that he had pushed the boy, who then fell against the fire. The boy however stated that Anderson had forced him upon the fire, but that he had managed to get off before being burned. The magistrate, stating that Anderson was fortunate that the boy had not been hurt, fined him one guinea.

A Victorian Fireplace. From the author's own collection.

19th April 1875

A disturbance in the Grassmarket on a Saturday night resulted in Andrew Padon appearing in the Police Court. Padon was accused of attacking a Carter named Monaghan with a razor, a revolver, a coal axe and a frying pan, in Crawford's Close. He was remitted to a higher court.

28th April 1875

Domestic Servant, Mary McLeod was charge on this date with an 'alleged concealment of pregnancy'. Evidence was given by a fellow servant that she had suspected McLeod, who was fifteen years old, was pregnant and it was alleged that on the 4th April she had given birth to a male child whilst the family and other servants were at church, the body of which was found in the garden. The case was remitted to a higher court.

17th June 1880

A young man named John Rodgers was charged with having attempted to commit suicide by climbing over the parapet of the Dean Bridge and hanging from it by the hands. The court was told that Rodgers, who had been teetotal for the last nine months, had attended a Wedding the previous night and had indulged rather freely in liquor.

24th November 1881

A charge of stealing overcoats landed Adam Skivving, Mary Ann Sinclair and Christina Wyse in court, following numerous complaints being received by the police of overcoats being stolen from the lobbies of their houses. It appears that the accused had entered the lobbies of houses throughout the city where the doors had been left open and helped themselves to the coats. On their apprehension, a considerable number of stolen articles were recovered.

15th June 1882

James Flynn, an old man, was imprisoned for 60 days for the theft of a purse. From the evidence given it appeared that the accused was observed by a boy of lifting the purse, which had been dropped by a lady in Brougham Street, and on being asked by the lady to return it, Flynn had told her that the boy had taken it. Flynn was however, taken to the police office, where the purse was discovered secreted in his stocking.

13th February 1885

Donald Graham McNair was sentenced on this date to 21 days imprisonment for having on various occasions stolen several sums of money from children in different parts of the city.

14th January 1886

Neglecting to remove snow from the pavements in front of their premises resulted in several shopkeepers appearing in the Police Court. The shopkeepers were admonished on this occasion, but advised that they would be liable to a penalty if there was any repeat.

27th January 1887

Juvenile beggars, Mary Connor and John Connor, aged nine and six years of age respectively, were charged at the Police Court with begging in

South Bridge. The children having run away from their parents, had travelled, concealed under the seat of a railway carriage, to Edinburgh. The father of the children stated that the girl had led the boy away and asked that she be sent to an industrial school, and the boy be liberated. A police inspector gave evidence that both the father and the mother had previously been convicted of begging. The Sheriff decided that it was in the interests of both children that they should be sent to an industrial school.

14th February 1887

On this date, Thomas Smith, who had been previously convicted for begging was again in court for the same offence. Smith, an out of work Clerk, represented himself and was sentenced to ten days imprisonment.

2nd April 1888

Elderly man George Bathgate pushed his way noisily in to the Police Court, despite an attempt being made by the officers to keep him out, and sat down on a bench reserved for policemen giving evidence, exclaiming to the officers "what's wrang wi' ye?". When he took his place at the bar, he pleaded not guilty to a charge of having 'uttered oaths, made use of abusive language' annoyed the shopkeeper and refused to leave the shop. It seems that Bathgate had entered the shop whilst drunk and after purchasing a half penny worth of milk, he began to swear and brandish his stick and had to be removed by the police. The charge having been found proven, he was fined £1 or the alternative of five days imprisonment. On being shown to the cells, Bathgate stated that he had the money in his pocket to pay the fine, but instead of going into the public part of the court, he ran alongside the bar where he was caught by officers. As he was taken into the cells, Bathgate shouted "You Blackguard!".

6th July 1889

The Police Court heard evidence in support of a charge of theft against an Edinburgh cab driver named John Cunningham. In the evidence given, it was shown that on a previous night two gentlemen were driven in a cab to Torphichen Street, of which Cunningham was on the box along with the driver. On arrival at the destination, one of the passengers had dropped a sovereign, which Cunningham was suspected to have picked up. Police officers attended and saw the missing sovereign drop from the harness with which Cunningham was said to have previously been tampering. Cunningham was sent to prison for ten days.

25th September 1890

A case described as an 'Interesting Case to Butchers' was heard in the Police Court on this date. Henry Rothel, a butcher in the Kirkgate, was charged with having exposed for eight hours a carcase of an animal outside the door, to the annoyance of passers by. The magistrate had visited the location to see for himself and took the view that although the carcases were hanging outside where people had to walk past, as they were not causing an obstruction, he found the case not proven.

3rd September 1891

A boy named David Adamson appeared at Leith Police Court on this date, charged with stealing apples from a garden. He was sentenced to ten days imprisonment and five years detention in a reformatory.

19th December 1892

A case reported as 'An Extraordinary Incident at Edinburgh Theatre Royal' was heard on this date. Robert Chisholm and John Candie were charged with having, in the gallery of the Theatre Royal, Broughton Street, 'uttered oaths, shouted, bawled, and annoyed and disturbed the audience, while a performance was taking place'. Candie pleaded guilty, whilst Chisholm stated that he was so drunk he couldn't remember any of it. The case was continued.

5th July 1894

Reckless use of a revolver resulted in James Kemp being fined the grand sum of £3, for having behaved in a 'disorderly manner' in South College Street and Potterrow, by presenting a loaded revolver at several persons.

3rd January 1895

Thomas Blackie was charged at the City Police Court, having on New Years Day, launched a savage attack on his brother George. Thomas had visited George on New Years Day and the pair had entered into an argument about horse betting. Both men then got up from their seats and started pushing each other about, when the accused bit a piece out of his brother's lip, which required five stitches. The magistrate characterised the assault as 'one which a dog would have committed' and fined him £1.

23rd June 1896

In the City Police Court, six girls who had escaped from the Dalry Reformatory appeared for sentence. Two of the girls, who had previously been convicted of the same offence, were sentenced to forty days imprisonment; another two, who had been found on Calton Hill in the company of a man, were sentenced to fourteen days imprisonment; and the remaining two were sentenced to ten days imprisonment. In their defence, it was stated that during the last eighteen months there had been a large amount of insubordination among the girls, which was attributed to a 'laxity of management' on the part of the officials, and a high turnover of staff.

1st April 1897

John Bell, 19 years old, described as a Grocer's Assistant, faced a charge of having ridden a bicycle 'furiously, recklessly and carelessly' in

Morningside Road, whereby the bicycle came into contact with Mary Edgar and knocked her down. The case was remitted to a higher court.

7th October 1898

David Dewar, a Railway Porter, having been observed by two detective officers, drinking from a beer barrel with a brass tube, was sentenced to 10 days imprisonment for the theft of the barrel from Leith Walk Station. The barrel contained 14 gallons of beer.

Chapter 2

Sheriff Court

The Function of the Sheriff Court

Lawnmarket

In 19th Century Edinburgh, the Sheriff Court was situated in the Lawnmarket. This court dealt with the majority of criminal and civil cases, however as the power of this court was limited, major crimes were usually remitted to the High Court, and civil cases which were of a more complex nature were usually dealt with by the Court of Session. The same still applies today, however a new Sheriff Court building now stands, and the old Sheriff Court building is now used as the High Court of Justiciary. As with the City Police Court, the Sheriff Court could deal cases under Summary Procedure, however its sentencing power was greater. The Sheriff Court however, also dealt with cases under the more serious Solemn Procedure, where the cases are heard by a Sheriff sitting with a jury. Any cases thought to be out with the sentencing scope of the Sheriff Court were remitted to the High Court.

Sheriff Court Cases in Victorian Edinburgh

14th December 1838

In the Sheriff Court on this date, a man described as 'a gentleman in this neighbourhood' was sued by one of his previous servants for the amount of a half year's wages. However, as he had left his employer's service before the agreed time, the Court decided that he had forfeited his wages.

13th December 1839

In the Sheriff Court, Michael Brodie, described as the head of 'a band of gipsies or tinkers', was tried for Malicious Mischief, where it was alleged that he had damaged the property of farmers in Granton, after being legally ejected from their area. Brodie was sentenced to two months imprisonment.

17th October 1840

Farm servants, John Richardson and Thomas Wight, were tried on a charge of 'furiously driving their carts on the highway' and assaulting two police constables, who challenged them over the offence. Richardson received a fine of 40s and Wight received a fine of 20s.

2nd April 1842

'Five young gentlemen' were brought before the court on a charge of having 'wickedly and maliciously broken a number of windows' on the previous Saturday night. The young men had driven in a drag from Edinburgh to Aberlady on the Saturday afternoon, and on their way back to Edinburgh they had stopped in a street which had recently been laid. Two of the men got out at this point and lifted a quantity of stones into the bottom of the drag, then proceeding home, they amused themselves by breaking a number of windows of households they were passing. The young men pleaded guilty and were fined £10 each, which was the highest amount the Sheriff could fine them.

7th August 1844

On this date, labourers Adam Davidson and Alexander Ramsay, found themselves in the Sheriff Court charged with stealing a bee hive containing honey from a garden at Saughton Hall. A handkerchief which had been dropped at the scene identified one of the thieves, with the property being recovered soon after. Both were sentenced to thirty days imprisonment.

14th November 1844

A Sheriff and Jury trial took place on this date, featuring a case in which a man had been charged with theft after receiving a surplus of money paid to him by the bank. Neil Cameron, a Journeyman Slater from Leith had went to the National Security Savings Bank of Edinburgh to withdraw the sum of £2, 3s, however the clerk had instead paid to him the sum of £23. The error was discovered by a teller at the close of the bank that day and the discrepancy in the books was traced to Cameron. As Cameron did not correct this mistake and instead kept the money, he found himself on trial for 'a wicked and felonious theft'. Suspicion had also been raised when Cameron had later that day walked into a Spirit Dealer's shop in Leith and asked for change of a £5 note. The evidence from all parties involved secured the verdict of 'guilty' and Cameron was imprisoned for four calendar months.

18th February 1846

Nine men were charged with assaulting various police constables while in the execution of their duty in Blackfriars Wynd, early on a Sunday morning the previous December. A Night Watchman, William Miller, whilst on his rounds, heard the voice of a female calling for assistance from Blackfriars Wynd. On entering the wynd, Millar saw that she was standing among a number of men who appeared to be involved in a scuffle. However, in order to reach them, Miller had to pass a group of labourers who were standing at the entrance of a passage leading to a public house, and in doing so he was struck down by some of the party and repeatedly kicked. As Miller's colleagues arrived to assist him, they were one by one, assaulted by the party, who by this time were armed with a poker, spade and axe. With the arrival of more police, the party were eventually overcome and apprehended. The jury found the charge not proven against two of the men, and the others who were found guilty, were sentenced to periods of imprisonment ranging from two to six months.

3rd July 1847

Attempting to leap upon one of the carriages of the Edinburgh and Glasgow Railway whilst it was going at speed, resulted in James McNeil, from the West Port, appearing in the Sheriff Court. Finding him guilty, the Sheriff fined McNeil 20s.

14th June 1848

Elizabeth McDonald was found guilty on this date of the theft of a piece of beef from a flesher in the Fleshmarket Close. She was sentenced to twelve months imprisonment.

27th August 1849

James Stevenson, an Underground Overman employed at Arniston Colliery, Edinburgh, was tried on this date on a charge of Culpable Homicide. The charge detailed that Stevenson had failed to see that the rope used for drawing boxes of coal up an inclined plane, was in good order and repair, and in sufficient working condition. The result of which had been that George Sneddon, a Collier working in the pit, had been caught by the knots on the rope and had been hurled against a crane in the area. Fortunately, Sneddon only sustained slight injury from this, however, as it seemed to be the insufficient rope that was to blame for this accident and as Stevenson did not repair or renew it, he was thought to be responsible for the unfortunate death of John Sommerville, who having been injured in exactly the same set of circumstances as Sneddon had been, died three days later, due to his injuries being more severe. The jury however, did not agree that Stevenson was to blame, and accordingly found him not guilty.

12th April 1850

A Sub-Postmaster, Robert Finlay, found himself in the dock on this date, accused of the misappropriation of money orders. The charge was that on the 5th November 1849, Finlay had taken two legitimately pre paid letters, put used stamps on them and wrote the words 'old stamp 2d' on the letters, thereby taxing the letters with a postage tax of twopence. Additionally, Finlay was charged with 'fraudulently and feloniously raising money for his own uses, which involved filling up a money order for £5, which he had stated had been paid by his wife, and sending it to a provision merchants to pay an account due by him. Finlay pleaded guilty to these charges and was sentenced to nine months imprisonment.

19th November 1850

Susan Wilson, who pleaded guilty to the theft of a double blanket from a loft in the house of James Spence, was sentenced to eight months imprisonment on this date.

18th February 1851

Martha Dickson pleaded guilty to 'falsehood, fraud, and wilful imposition'. The circumstances were that on various occasions she had received provisions from the Parochial Board on the pretence of collecting them on behalf of a man named Lenny, who was a pauper. Dickson was sentenced to ten months imprisonment.

10th February 1852

Omnibus Driver, Alexander Carse, pleaded guilty in the Sheriff Court of a culpable neglect of duty. Carse, who was in charge of an omnibus at the time, deserted the horses, whereby they set of at a 'furious rate' down the North Bridge and collided violently with Alex Sanson, a Tailor, severely injuring him. Carse was fined the sum of £10 or the alternative of thirty days imprisonment.

29th May 1855

On this date in the Sheriff Court, James Robertson, a Shoemaker, was charged with stabbing Alexander Gibson, also a Shoemaker, with a knife. The jury found the charge proven, however as it appeared the accused had been greatly provoked, they recommended leniency for the prisoner. As a result, Robertson was ordered to keep the peace for six months under a penalty of £5.

3rd November 1855

A charge of perjury resulted in a sentence of twelve months imprisonment for labourer, Andrew Colston, from the Pleasance. Colston had sworn that he had not been supplied with drink by spirit dealer, Cochrane, after eleven o'clock at night. Cochrane, however, had been found guilty of keeping an open house after this hour of night and it was established that Colston's evidence was false.

31st May 1856

William Proven and David Grierson, who had pleaded guilty to stealing a piece of lead pipe, were sentenced in the Sheriff Court on this date. As Proven had a previous conviction, he was sentenced to nine months imprisonment, three of them with hard labour. Grierson was sentenced to thirty days imprisonment.

15th June 1857

On this day, Charles Young, a baker, Bernard O'Hara, a plumber, and David Moir, a flesher, were charged with assault and breach of the peace for a disturbance on the Edinburgh Fast Day, 23rd April 1857. They were accused of attacking and assaulting a police constable and other persons within the inn at Roslin, using sticks and other weapons. Young received eighteen months imprisonment with hard labour, O'Hara received sixty days imprisonment and Moir was admonished.

20th February 1860

Two very different cases heard before the same Sheriff on this date received remarkably similar sentences: Michael Denaney who assaulted a woman with a stick, to the danger of her life, received four months imprisonment; whilst Ann Davidson who stole a pair of boots, was sentenced to three months imprisonment.

4th April 1861

Peter Rugan, a Blacksmith, was charged in the Edinburgh Sheriff Court with giving false information to a registrar regarding the birth of a child. Rugan denied the charge and the case went to trial. From the evidence given, it seems that Rugan's sister gave birth to an illegitimate child the previous September, however Rugan, on registering the birth, told the registrar that his sister was a married woman whose husband resided in Greenock. Having been found guilty, Rugan was sentenced to three months imprisonment, with the Sheriff informing him that if he had not taken a lenient view of the case, a sentence of seven years transportation could have been imposed.

26th March 1863

A case of 'Highway Robbery' was heard at the Sheriff Court on this date. John MacIntyre, a private in the second battalion of the 25th Regiment, stationed in Edinburgh Castle, was charged with attacking and assaulting George Simpson by striking him repeatedly on the head, with intent to rob him, whilst he was on the public road by Portobello. George Simpson gave evidence that he had been accosted by the accused and two other soldiers and had received blows about the head by the accused, who was chasing after him. Simpson then managed to strike MacIntyre on the face a few times with his walking stick, at which point MacIntyre gave up his pursuit. Simpson also stated that as he gave the three men no provocation whatsoever, their motive for attacking him must have been robbery. It was confirmed that when MacIntyre was apprehended he had cuts on the face consistent with the blows from the stick. The jury found MacIntyre guilty and he was sentenced to eighteen months imprisonment with hard labour.

5th December 1864

A case appeared in the Sheriff Summary Court on this date featuring the Reverend Dr Guthrie and a boar. A Gardner, Alex Dods was charged with endangering life, in not keeping a boar belonging to him under proper charge. Dr Guthrie had reported that whilst travelling with his son in a horse drawn vehicle at Greenend, when the enraged boar attacked and wounded the horse. He stated that initially he thought that the horse was not much hurt and so they drove on until they came to Liberton Manse, when they discovered that the horse had received a gash in the thigh which was four inches long and an inch and a half deep, in addition to a wound on the horses stomach. Evidence was given by witnesses for both parties and the charge was ultimately found 'not proven'.

13th May 1867

At the Sheriff Court on this date, Bernard Murphy, a Shoemaker, faced a charge of deserting his wife and family, which resulted in them receiving poor relief from the City Parish of Edinburgh. Murphy was sentenced to sixty days imprisonment.

27th February 1868

A 'Pious Fraud' landed Irishmen Timothy O'Donovan in the Sheriff Court. It seems O'Donovan had told various persons in Edinburgh that he was suffering great persecution from priests, as he had converted from Roman Catholicism to the Protestant religion, and that he desired to print a book detailing this persecution. Additionally, O'Donovan told people that he wanted to build a school, and as a result of these deceptions, he received substantial contributions. The case was continued.

6th January 1870

Stealing eight hams resulted in Andrew Dow, residing in the Lawnmarket, appearing in the Sheriff Court on this date. Dow had broken into the cellar of a grocer in Fountainbridge, where he had procured the hams. He was sentenced to six months imprisonment.

18th October 1871

Assaults on the police resulted in James Mitchell appearing in the Edinburgh Sheriff Court, accused of striking two policemen on the face and head, and additionally striking one of them with a gun. After much conflicting evidence, Mitchell was convicted only of the second charge, for which he was sentenced to thirty days imprisonment.

14th November 1872

John Lawson appeared in the Sheriff Court on this date, charged with stealing 11 pairs of stockings from the shop door of a Draper. Lawson was found guilty by the jury, and as he had a previous conviction, he was sentenced to ten months imprisonment.

6th January 1873

An assault during the festive period led to William Toollan appearing before the Sheriff on this date. From the evidence it appeared that on New Year's Day, after the prisoner and four other persons had consumed eight bottles of whisky and several quarts of ale in a house in Cannongate, it was reported that he 'became outrageous', and severely beat a woman named Katherine McQueen, who was one of the party. He was sentenced to fifteen days imprisonment with hard labour.

16th February 1874

In the Sheriff Summary Court on this date, Andrew Howieson, a Joiner, was charged with a contravention of the Vaccination (Scotland) Act, in which it was alleged that Howieson had refused to allow his infant daughter to be vaccinated. Pleading guilty, Howieson stated that he considered one of his other children to have been poisoned as a consequence of the vaccination. He was fined 35s or the option of ten days incarceration.

18th May 1874

Another case which resulted in a not proven verdict was that of Thomas Neill, a Collier, who had been charged under the Master and Servant Act, with leaving the employment of Messrs Deans & Moore without giving a fortnights notice.

5th September 1874

A man and a woman described as 'tramps' were charged with having stolen articles of wearing apparel from an outhouse at Torsonce South Lodge. The lodge was occupied by a coachman and his wife, who had heard the gate open and then a noise in their outhouse after midnight. Having looked out of the window, they saw a man and a woman passing by and later discovered the items missing. On the articles being found in the possession of the two accused, the male prisoner said that he knew nothing about them until he saw them in his wife's hands in the morning.

The Sheriff finding the charge proven, sentenced both of them to thirty days in jail.

22nd February 1875

Two young men named Andrew Millar and John Wilson, and a young woman named Frances Stewart, were charged at the Sheriff Summary Court with robbing a miner of £2, 12s and 6d while he was asleep in the female prisoner's house. They were also charged with assaulting the man at the same location by knocking him down and kicking him on several parts of the body. The case went to trial and all three were convicted, with Millar being sentenced to sixty days imprisonment with hard labour, and Wilson and Stewart to thirty days each.

27th May 1875

An unusual case was heard in the Sheriff Court on this date. The background to which was that about a month previous, a Miss Tyler, living in Morningside, became alarmed by a series of annoyances which occurred during the night at her house. These annoyances took the form of the loud ringing of the door bells and the breaking of the glass windows. The police, having been informed, were unable to discover what had happened and after these incidents occurred on several nights, a number of officers in plain clothes were sent to keep a watch night and day. This continued for three weeks, with more strange events occurring, such as the upsetting of tables and chairs, without the police being able to discover the cause. Additionally, Miss Tyler's servant frequently showed marks of having been violently struck by stones coming through the windows. However it was established that she was in fact the culprit in this case, and when the police had been watching one end of the house, she broke the windows at the other and vice versa, keeping them on a wild goose chase. This young woman, Violet Hall, described as 'rational looking' gave no reason for her behaviour, but admitted her guilt. She was sentenced to 60 days imprisonment with hard labour.

11th October 1877

A case of 'Housebreaking by a Policeman' was heard in the Sheriff Court. Alexander Macpherson was charged with having, while in the Edinburgh City Police Force, and on duty in Shandwick Place, broken into a cellar by opening the door with a false key. From this cellar, which was occupied by John Heron, a spirit dealer, Macpherson stole two bottles containing porter. It was stated during the proceedings, that he had been a policeman for 17 years, and that during that time he had shown good character. The Sheriff however, said that Macpherson was guilty of the 'worst crimes that a man could commit' and imprisoned him for nine months.

21st April 1879

On this date, a judicial examination took place in the Sheriff Court, in which Edward Fegan and John Donnolly, both Navvies, appeared on a charge of murder. Both accused had attended a public house in the village of Stobsmill on the previous Saturday night, along with other acquaintances, and during the course of the evening a disturbance arose in which Michael McLaughlin, a young man who was part of their group, was struck and kicked, and later died of a fracture of the skull.

4th August 1880

John Hussack, appearing from the prison of Edinburgh, was charged with the cruel and unnatural treatment and wilful and culpable neglect of his two children, both boys, who were aged seven and three years old. The charge detailed that at their house in Charlotte Street, Leith, Hussack assaulted the children by striking them with his fists and with a stick and twisting the arm of the elder boy. The result of the assaults being fractures to the arms and legs of the children, which as medical help was not sought for them to be set, were likely to result in deformities of their limbs. Evidence was given by witnesses, including a surgeon from the workhouse who had examined the children, and confirmed the presence of fractures and bruises and evidence of starvation. The jury unanimously found the accused guilty, and he was sentenced to ten months imprisonment.

15th June 1882

A Sheriff and Jury trial took place on this date, involving a man named David Paterson Boyd, who was charged with having stolen on various occasions between July 1881 and January 1882, nine engravings and 296 Christmas cards from the shop of Mr Hill, Printseller, Castle Street, Edinburgh, who had employed Boyd as a Clerk. The value of the stolen property was stated to be about £37 and Boyd was also accused of sending the prints to London to be sold by auction.

21st February 1884

A young lad named George Robinson pleaded guilty to snatching a card case from a lady's pocket on the 31st January 1884. As he had been previously convicted four times, he was sent to prison for 15 months with hard labour. On leaving the dock, the prisoner shouted to some of his friends "cheer up!".

10th April 1884

On this date, a charge of Bigamy was heard in the Sheriff Court. Thomas Downie, a middle aged man, pleaded guilty to the charge, in which he had married Jane Macdonald, a domestic servant, whilst still being married to his wife of eight years, Mary Brady. Downie was sentenced to eight months imprisonment.

Also on this date, Peter Morgan, described as 'a rough looking man', was sentenced to nine months imprisonment, having assaulted a woman in a lodging house in the Grassmarket by knocking her down and fracturing two of her ribs by kicking her.

Grassmarket, Edinburgh © Peter Stubbs, Edinphoto

8th December 1884

In the Sheriff Summary Court, two guards employed by the North British Railway Company, were convicted of stealing a quantity of whisky from a cask in the course of its transit between Castlecarry and Corstorphine stations. They were each sentenced to 20 days imprisonment.

14th February 1885

On this date, a young man named John Gibson was charged with having attempted to ravish a girl whilst in a railway carriage between Edinburgh and Glasgow on 22nd November 1884. Gibson pleaded not guilty, however after the evidence had been presented, the jury returned a guilty verdict and he was sentenced to six months imprisonment.

3rd September 1886

A case of 'Reset' was tried in the Sheriff Court, involving a man named George Sharp, who had stolen a silver watch and chain with locket from a mason in an Edinburgh public house. Sharp had written to the Sheriff trying the case, expressing repentance and his desire to begin a new life. He was sentenced to six months imprisonment.

1st November 1888

James Gilroy, described as 'a miserable looking old man' was found guilty of having, on the 13th September, stolen an overcoat and a knife from a house in Portobello. He was sentenced to twelve months imprisonment

7th January 1890

George Brown, who had previous convictions, was sent to prison for 60 days with hard labour for an assault on his wife. Brown carried out the assault after returning to the house, where his wife was lying ill, and asking her for money, to which she refused. Brown gave the excuse that 'the drink at the New Year must have been very bad'.

3rd September 1891

An elderly woman named Mary Strain was charged with wilfully ill treating and neglecting her daughter, Jane Strain, aged three years, leading to the girl becoming emaciated and exhausted, and dying as a result. Strain pleaded not guilty and a trial date was set.

30th June 1892

A sentence of six months imprisonment was given to Robert Mathieson, who pleaded guilty to breaking into churches in Leith and stealing two bottles of wine and eight biscuits.

17th January 1893

A peculiar case of Culpable Homicide was heard in the Sheriff Court on this date. Mary Dunnigan, who had been attempting to throw a metal watch stand at her husband, with whom she often quarrelled, missed her husband, and instead struck her daughter, Alice Dunnigan, with it. Mary Dunnigan took her daughter to the dispensary for medical assistance and was advised to take her to the Infirmary. However, she did not and the child only arrived at the Infirmary when she was taken there by the police. The Sheriff in this case passed a sentence of eight months imprisonment.

Edinburgh Royal Infirmary © Peter Stubbs, Edinphoto

3rd April 1893

Destitute John Hodgkin was sent to prison for three months for having set fire to a stack of straw on Bank Farm, Corstorphine. Hodgkin had stated that he only set the fire in order that he would be sent to prison and therefore get food.

7th April 1893

The case of Reset by a man named Alex Ross was tried on this date. The circumstances were that a ship's carpenter, Joseph Aunoldick, having been paid off from his vessel in Leith, went to a public house where he met the accused and bought him a drink. The seaman then proceeded to a tailor shop where he bought some clothes, and later attended another public house where he met two women. Having accompanied the women to one of their houses, one of the women took his purse from his pocket and threw it to the other, who rushed down the stairs with it, and passed it to the accused. All three in this case were sentenced to six months imprisonment.

4th August 1894

On this date, a case was tried involving two people described as 'a brutal father and mother'. William Holding and his wife, Robina Holding, were charged with cruelly ill treating and neglecting their five children. The eldest of the children was described as being 'an idiot' and had been kept all his life in a recumbent position in a cradle. Sheriff Blair, in summing up described this as a 'very, very bad case' and looking at the long period during which the couple had neglected their children, the way in which they had neglected the helpless condition of their eldest son, and the tender ages of their younger children, he commented that he must pass severe sentences. William Holding was sentenced to 18 months imprisonment and Robina Holding to 15 months imprisonment.

4th November 1895

A 65 year old man, Thomas Campbell, pleaded guilty to a charge of resetting a stolen watch in a pawn office, and was sentenced to four months imprisonment. Campbell's previous convictions showed that during his life he had served sentences which all together amounted to a total of 30 years spent in prison.

17th April 1896

Archibald Philips was sentenced to three months imprisonment for stabbing his brother on the head with a knife. It was stated that the accused had asked his invalid mother for money, at which point his brother intervened and was stabbed by the accused.

3rd August 1896

Counterfeiting four coins to represent shillings landed William Simpson in the dock. Having then uttered the coins on four occasions, Simpson was sentenced to nine months imprisonment.

31st July 1897

A case of a brutal assault was heard in the Sheriff Court on this date. Jas Begley pleaded guilty to having on 29th June, in his house in Scott's Close, Edinburgh, assaulted his wife, Mary Begley. Jas and Mary Begley had been out drinking together and when they returned to the house a quarrel had started. It was detailed that Jas Begley had grabbed his wife by the throat, compressing her throat and also kicked her on the head, damaging her left eye, which ruptured and had to be taken out on her arrival at the Royal Infirmary. Having five previous convictions, he was sentenced to nine months imprisonment for this crime.

A typical Edinburgh close © Peter Stubbs, Edinphoto

10th August 1897

The case of a theft by a Laudanum drinker was heard on this date. A woman named Rae, pleaded guilty to thirteen charges of theft from shop doors, the articles stolen being mainly boots and shoes. Rae had previously been convicted of theft on one occasion, and her defence agent stated that she had become strongly addicted to Laudanum and the thefts had been committed whilst she was under its influence. Rae was sentenced to four months imprisonment.

10th February 1899

Middle aged man, Thomas Dowling was charged with seven acts of theft of Christmas parcels from the Post Office authorities between 18th

December and 31st December the previous year, whilst he had been employed by them to collect parcels at the branch post offices during the Christmas season. Dowling's method was to cover up the original address on the parcel and then address it to himself, in order that he would receive the parcels, rather than their intended recipients. He was sentenced to twelve months imprisonment.

1st October 1900

A warrant was granted for the apprehension of Landed proprietor, Thomas Greer, who failed to attend at the court on this date, having been accused of gross indecency in a lavatory of the Waverley Station, Edinburgh.

Chapter 3

High Court of Justiciary

The Function of the High Court of Justiciary

The High Court of Justiciary, now situated in the Lawnmarket, was and still is the supreme criminal court of Scotland, dealing with serious criminal matters, such as Murder. High Court trials were held before a judge and jury, however in addition to trials, it presided over any criminal appeal cases from the High Court and the lower courts. The High Court of Justiciary could give very lengthy prison sentences and in the Victorian era, could also give the sentence of death by hanging. An alternative to these sentences was 'Transportation', sometimes called 'Penal Transportation'. This popular court disposal was the deporting of convicted criminals to the colonies either for life or for a set period of time. Transportation, which was usually the result of a High Court trial, was seen as the humane alternative to execution, however as we will see in this chapter, this sentence was often given for fairly petty offences. The sentencing of people to Transportation ended in the late 1860s.

High Court of Justiciary Cases in Victorian Edinburgh

16th March 1839

Peter Lays, a farm steward, residing in Morrison Street, appeared at the bar accused of assaulting a young man named Rintoul by pushing him off one of the carriages of the train between Musselburgh and Edinburgh. Rintoul fell under the wheels of another carriage and received a fracture to one of his thighs and various other injuries. Lays was found guilty by the jury, however it was accepted that he had no premeditated malice against Rintoul, and the judge found the railway company more to blame, as overloading their carriages with people was a common practice. Lays was therefore sentenced to three months imprisonment.

11th November 1839

Shoemaker, Alexander McDonald was placed at the bar, charged with committing a criminal assault upon a twelve year old girl. McDonald pleaded not guilty and the case was tried with closed doors. The jury found a verdict of not proven and McDonald was dismissed from the bar. This case had attracted considerable interest as it was the second time McDonald had been liberated, with the first trial, which was also on indictment, taking place after him being arrested having fled the country.

12th January 1840

Charles Dewar was found guilty on this date of the robbery of premises on the North Bridge. Dewar was the son of a builder who had earned a considerable fortune by his trade and built Dewar Place. Charles Dewar, as a result of his father's death, had inherited what was described as 'an ample fortune' but had squandered it in taverns and gambling houses, leaving he and his wife in poverty. It was also brought to light that whilst Dewar was in prison awaiting his trial, he was found to have secreted portions of rope and hid them within his cell in order to attempt an escape.

7th July 1841

Fourteen year old Peter Gilmore pleaded not guilty to a charge of stealing a number of articles from a house in Royal Terrace. Gilmore who was described as being 'habit and repute a thief', and had previously been convicted of theft. The jury found him guilty on clear evidence and prior to sentencing the court was told of Gilmore's background. Losing his parents when he was young, he had been sent to the Charity Workhouse of the city, from where he was then apprenticed to a handloom weaver. Gilmore however had left this occupation on account of being compelled to work from five in the morning until nine at night, at which point he went to sea. Alleging 'ill usage' whilst he was at sea, Gilmore also left this work and fell into a criminal lifestyle. Considering all of this, the judge decided to give him another chance to 'reclaim his character' and change his 'idle disposition', by sentencing him to eighteen months imprisonment.

9th November 1841

Seven years transportation was the sentence given to Mary Aitken on this date, for the theft of two crystal tumblers.

On the same day, William Sweenie was given the same sentence for the theft of dried fish and some ale.

6th January 1842

Four Edinburgh University students pleaded guilty on this date to a charge of 'being engaged in fighting a duel' in a park near the Grange Loan. Luckily this duel only resulted in one of the students receiving a would to the thigh, however the judge sentenced all four of them to two months imprisonment.

8th November 1843

Resetting eight umbrellas led to John Russell and Robert Lawson appearing in court. It appeared the umbrellas had previously been stolen from a shop in the South Bridge. Both accused in this case, had previous convictions for theft, however Lawson was sentenced to six months imprisonment, whilst Russell received seven years transportation.

8th January 1844

Alexander McDonald pleaded guilty to a charge of theft from a stable in Drummond Street. Having been previously convicted of theft, he was sentenced to 7 years transportation.

9th January 1844

James Brogan, charged with having wickedly and feloniously used and uttered a counterfeit coin, knowing it to be false. Brogan pleaded not guilty, however, on hearing the evidence of the nine witnesses which were called, the jury found him guilty and he was sentenced to ten years transportation.

16th May 1844

Cabinet Maker, Thomas Henderson, convicted of the theft of a plank of mahogany from a wood yard in East Broughton Place, found himself sentenced to seven years transportation, having had previous convictions for theft.

On the same date, Mary Campbell or Crawford was sentenced to seven years transportation, having been convicted of the theft of a shawl from a house.

Arthur Wilson, also convicted of theft, received seven years transportation for stealing items from a cart.

19th May 1844

On this date, stealing a silk handkerchief resulted in a sentence of seven years transportation for Janet Campbell.

Another sentence of seven years transportation was given to Thomas Fyfe, after stealing five spoons and four forks from a house in Picardy Place.

24th July 1845

Mary McKenzie and Lillian Leggat were charged with having stolen a pair of shoes, a blue cloth jacket and two vests from Mary McKenzie's son James. Both women were described as 'habitual thieves', and the jury, on hearing the evidence in the case, found them both guilty. McKenzie was sentenced to seven years transportation and Leggat to ten years transportation.

10th February 1847

Habitual thieves, James Stewart and Robert Kirk received sentences of seven years transportation, after being convicted of the theft of several pieces of canvas and some culinary articles.

8th November 1847

James Edey, a labourer, was placed at the bar, charged with the crime of Culpable Homicide. Edey, who pleaded not guilty, was accused of attacking and assaulting John Scott, the Edinburgh Executioner, and causing his death. The charge detailed that on the 12th August, Edey, either in or near the Old Fleshmarket Close, or in the Cowgate, or in the shop of a spirit dealer there, struck Scott one or more blows on his head or neck. Edey pleaded not guilty and the case went to trial. Evidence was given by several witnesses, including shop owners, who stated that they had seen Edey in a state of intoxication and acting it what was described as 'an outrageous manner', approach Scott, verbally abuse him, strike him and then follow him as he attempted to get away and strike him further times. The jury took only five minutes to find the accused guilty.

26th January 1848

Stealing a bridle and some other articles from a stable, resulted in seven years transportation for William Mason.

Police Constables Henderson Smith and James Connor also found themselves in court on this date, charged with the theft of money from a house in Leith Street, occupied by a spirit dealer. They were found guilty by the jury and were each sentenced to ten years transportation, with the judge commenting that the sentences would have been greater had he wanted to make an example of them.

16th March 1848

The theft of a pair of boots from a house in Cumberland Street, gave Ronald Marshall the sentence of seven years transportation.

14th March 1849

Mary Bone, Henry Grant and Elizabeth Henderson were all placed at the bar, charged with having stolen a watch from a young man, whilst in a house in Leith Wynd. They pleaded not guilty, but after much evidence had been given the jury found the charge proven and all three were sentenced to ten years transportation.

6th January 1851

Mary Finnon was charged on this date with child murder, the circumstances of which being that she cast her new born child into a river, having first attached a heavy stone to the child's neck. Finnon pleaded guilty to the lesser crime of culpable homicide and was sentenced to transportation for life.

22nd July 1852

Another woman accused of child murder appeared in court on this date. Evidence was given that Mary Paterson had delivered a female child, which was afterwards found to have been strangled. Paterson pleaded guilty to the lesser charge of concealment of pregnancy and was sentenced to twelve months imprisonment.

15th June 1857

On this date, Madeline Smith was indicted on three counts: the first two counts charging her with attempting to murder Pierre L'Angelier, by administering arsenic to him on two separate occasions; the third count charging her with his murder, again by arsenic poisoning. A total of 89 witnesses were called by the prosecution in this case, consisting of close friends of the deceased, medical gentlemen and chemists, relatives of the accused and domestics staff employed by Smith and L'Angelier. The jury, after deliberating, were divided in their opinion, with five in favour of a verdict of guilty, and ten for not proven.

26th March 1859

Margaret McDonald stood trial on this date, charged with Child Murder. McDonald was accused of administering the poison, oxalic acid, to her child and afterwards taking a dose of the same poison herself, in an attempt to commit suicide. Her defence was that she had thought she was merely giving the child salt, and had no intention to cause harm. During the trial, the scenario painted was that McDonald had been promised by the child's father that he would marry her, however it appears that he changed his mind, which meant that McDonald, as an unmarried mother, unable to keep her job, inevitably had to enter the workhouse, where she had the baby. The jury, taking just fifteen minutes to deliberate, decided that a verdict of guilty for the lesser crime of Culpable Homicide was more appropriate.

21st February 1860

In the High Court on this date was a case of 'Assault by Throwing Muriatic Acid'. John Watling Barland, a druggist, was placed at the bar accused of assaulting cab driver Henry Shaw by throwing a quantity of muriatic acid upon his face, with the intent to main and disfigure him. It seems there had been a dispute in the street between the two about an unpaid fare which Shaw insisted Barland owed him from a year ago. Barland was then seen to go into his shop and mix something which was described as having 'smoke ascending from it'. Barland was then seen by witnesses to throw the mixture over Shaw exclaiming "there's your shilling!". Several persons then came to Shaw's assistance, applying buttermilk to his very painful and red face. The medical evidence given was that if the buttermilk had not been applied, the injuries could have been very serious, however it seems that this application had completely neutralised the acid. Barland, who stated that he had been very drunk at the time and had no recollection of the incident, was sentenced to nine months imprisonment.

24th February 1868

Francis Murlhair was placed at the bar on this date charged with stealing a quantity of 'wearing apparel' and bed clothes from a shop in the city. He was sentenced to seven years penal servitude.

18th May 1869

Stealing a roll of bacon from a grocer's shop in Charlotte Street, led to William Potter appearing in the High Court. As he had previously convicted of theft, Potter was sentenced to seven years penal servitude.

10th January 1870

Seven men were charged at the High Court of Justiciary with the crimes of mobbing and rioting, murder, and assault to the severe injury of the person. The indictment against them stated that on the 18th September 1869, whilst part of a large 'mob of rioters and evil disposed persons', they assembled at the house of James Docherty, a labourer, for the purpose of assaulting and maltreating certain persons within the house, who the mob believed to be Roman Catholics. They were also accused of conducting themselves in a 'riotous, tumultuous and menacing manner', kicking and forcing the door of the house open, attacking the persons inside and dragging James Docherty outside, where he was knocked to the ground and kicked violently on the head, resulting in his death. The jury, taking some time to deliberate, returned a verdict of 'not proven'.

26th January 1872

Selina Augusta Borgen, from Sweden, pleaded guilty to stealing a desk containing £40 from a house in Norton Place, Edinburgh. Prior to sentencing, it was stated that Borgen had came to Edinburgh in search of employment as a domestic servant, but due to inexperience in 'Scotch domestic service', she had not managed to secure a position. Additionally, as she had missed the last steamer of the season to Sweden, she had become stranded in Edinburgh without means to support herself. It was also stated that her previous character had been very good, and the Swedish Consul had promised to ensure that she returned home. However despite these factors, the court passed the severe sentence of five years penal servitude.

3rd March 1873

Cab Driver, John McDonald was accused of the crime of writing and sending a threatening letter to a person in Edinburgh for the purpose of extorting money. McDonald pleaded not guilty but after evidence had been given the jury unanimously found him guilty and he was sentenced to six months imprisonment.

10th May 1873

Administering laudanum to a child 'of tender years ' to the imminent danger of life was the charge Margaret Welsh appeared on in the High Court on this date. Welsh was accused of giving about sixty drops of laudanum to her illegitimate child, which was eight months old at the time. Pleading guilty to a lesser charge, she was sentenced to twelve months imprisonment.

13th October 1874

Appearing from the Calton jail, Thomas Heriot was charged with theft by housebreaking, having broken into the store of Craiglockhart Poorhouse and taken a pair of trousers, some moleskin cloth, cotton lining and canvas. The jury found Heriot guilty and having previous convictions, he was sentenced to ten years penal servitude.

Craiglockhart Poorhouse. From the author's own collection.

14th October 1874

Seventy year old James Crichton found himself placed at the bar on this date, charged with Murder. The indictment detailed that on the 25th or 26th July 1874 at his house in Paul Street, Edinburgh, he assaulted Ann Maxwell or Ritchie by kicking her on the head and face, and striking her on the head with a piece of broken chair, resulting in her death. Crichton pleaded not guilty and the principal witness for the defence was his granddaughter, Elizabeth Crichton, 11 years of age. Elizabeth told the court that on the night Anna died, her grandfather and Anna had been drinking and that prior to going to bed, Elizabeth had seen Anna sleeping on the floor and could see that she was breathing. Elizabeth then stated that she had witnessed her grandfather attempting to pick Ann up from the floor, but that she kept falling and on one occasion hit her head on the stone floor. Seeing her grandfather then strike Anna on the face,

Elizabeth asked him why he had done that, to which he replied "to waken her to get her into bed". The jury, by a majority, found the case not proven.

27th February 1877

Henry Clarke, described as 'a smart, intelligent-looking man, approaching middle age, was placed at the bar on a charge of murder. The details of the indictment were that in the High Street, Clarke attacked and assaulted John Rush, a barber's assistant, who resided with his mother in the Cannongate, by stabbing him on the neck with a pair of scissors. Clarke initially pleaded not guilty, but on the advice of his counsel, withdrew this and put in a plea of culpable homicide. The details which emerged were that the scissors were in Clarke's hand accidentally and that he had actually aimed to strike another person who had provoked him, but who had moved out of the way of the blow, resulting in Rush being struck. It also emerged that Clarke was in a state of intoxication at the time. The judge took all this into account and addressed Clarke, stating "if you are a man of any good feeling at all, you will remember with pain, and grave and deep distress as long as you live, that your drunken hands killed on the spot, a lad of eighteen'. Clarke was sentenced to eighteen months imprisonment and warned to abandon his drunken habits.

18th June 1881

In the Appeal Court, Mr Blackie, an Edinburgh Spirit Merchant, sought to suspend a conviction against him that he had received in the Police Court. The conviction had been for selling a quantity of spirits less than two gallons, in breach of his certificate. Blackie's argument was that the conviction was irrelevant, due to the fact that he held a licence, and further that he had been entrapped into selling the quantity specified (one pint) by a female turnkey in the service of the police. The court, without giving reason, quashed the conviction in this case and awarded seven guineas of expenses.

30th August 1889

John Hamilton Gray Mitchell, who had previously pleaded guilty to forging bank notes, was sentenced to seven years penal servitude. Mitchell was 74 years of age.

16th December 1889

Peter Campbell was charged on this date with the murder of a woman by assaulting her with a cleaver. Campbell tendered a plea of culpable homicide and was sentenced to 10 years penal servitude.

12th December 1892

On this date, David Kane, described as 'a young, good looking fellow', was charged with the murder of his wife in their house in Milne's Court, Lawnmarket, Edinburgh. The charge detailed that Kane had 'struck her with a hatchet, kicked her and murdered her'. Kane tendered a plea of culpable homicide, which was rejected, and the case went to trial. Mrs Brady, the mother of the deceased, gave evidence in great distress, stating that her daughter had previously complained to her about being 'ill used' by Kane and that she had seen him the worse of drink on the afternoon of the incident. The next morning, Kane reported that his wife was dead and the deceased's brother, John Brady called for the police. The two doctors who carried out the post mortem gave evidence that there were forty abrasions on her body, and that the cause of death was shock. The also stated that her jaw had been shattered and a piece of it was detached, consistent with a severe blow. Additionally, one of her ribs which had been fractured, had punctured her left lung, and as she had been a woman who was not of 'strong constitution', her right lung had been unable to cope. Witnesses for the defence however, consisting of Kane's father and sister, gave evidence that Mrs Kane had been often drunk and would stay away from her home for two or three days at a time, due to her drunken habits. The Lord Justice Clerk, in summing up, stated that this was "one of those sad cases which from time to time came before the court; one of those cases in which two persons who gave way to drink unfortunately found themselves one dead and the other placed at the bar charged with the death". The jury, after an absence of fifteen minutes, found Kane guilty of Culpable Homicide. He was sentenced to 15 years imprisonment.

Lawnmarket, Edinburgh © Peter Stubbs, Edinphoto

7th June 1897

At the Appeal Court, David Syme, a Dairyman, sought a suspension of his conviction in the Police Court for 'wilfully and maliciously' scratching and defacing the doors of nine houses in Manor Place and various localities in that district, for which he had received a fine. Syme's grounds for seeking a suspension were that the proceedings of the magistrates had been 'incompetent, irregular, illegal and oppressive', as in the course of the trial, the evidence was conflicting as to whether the marks had been made by a corkscrew or a packing needle, and to demonstrate, marks had been made on a board using both, resulting in the proceedings being conducted in laughter. The appeal court in this case was of the opinion that there was not sufficient ground for quashing the conviction, and suspension was refused, with expenses awarded against the complainer.

Chapter 4

Notorious Cases and Executions

Public Execution, Edinburgh early 19th Century

3rd April 1844

Execution of James Bryce

In the presence of an immense crowd of spectators, thought to number 20,000 to 30,000, James Bryce was executed for the murder of his brother in law, John Geddes. Bryce had been brought over from the Calton Jail to the Lock-up House, about four o'clock the previous afternoon, in a hackney coach. The erection of the gallows began at eleven o'clock that night. The gallows were placed immediately at the top of Libberton's Wynd, with the steps to the mouth of the close, and the front of the scaffold facing up the Lawnmarket. This execution, being the first one in Edinburgh in four years, seemed to have attracted a great deal of interest. As early as six o'clock the next morning, a considerable crowd had already gathered, and as time wore on, on this wet April morning, more and more spectators joined the crowd, which by eight o'clock had become a dense mass of people, apparently consisting mostly of women and young persons. This mass stretched a considerable distance up the Lawnmarket and along George IV Bridge, whilst the windows in the vicinity, the roofs of houses, and every other available spot, were thronged with spectators. It was reported that Bryce had slept little the night before, and spent most of his time reading the Scriptures, assisted by the Chaplain of the jail. At the necessary time, Baillies Wilkie and Gray, in their official vestments, proceeded to the Lock up, where the convict was delivered over to their custody. On the arrival of the Magistrates, the three first verses of Psalm were sung, followed by a prayer, to which Bryce appeared to listen 'with the greatest reverence'. At exactly half past eight the procession left the Lock up and came up

Libberton's Wynd to the scaffold, Bryce being supported on either side by Chaplains. He proceeded up the stairs of the scaffold with firmness, occasionally glancing at the assembled crowd of spectators. After further prayer, the Chaplains shook hands with Bryce and then left, allowing the executioner, who had been brought from Glasgow, to proceed. Bryce was then placed on the drop, the rope adjusted and the cap drawn over his face. He was given a handkerchief to signal when he was ready, and on doing so, he was hanged. His death apparently occurred in a few seconds, but his body was allowed to hang for about half an hour, after which it was cut down and lowered into a coffin. The body was firstly taken to the Lock up, then taken over to the jail later in the day, where in accordance with his sentence, he was buried within the grounds of the jail.

The day before his execution, Bryce had made the following statement and confession:

"I was born in the parish of Ratho, and I am, I think, forty three or forty four years of age. My father was a shoemaker. I was put to school when about six years old, and remained at it for about five years, but was frequently away from it in summer herding cows. I was not attentive when at school, and often grieved my parents, who often warned me, and did all they could to make me do right; but I did not take their advice. My father was a sober and good man, and when I was at home took me to church or meeting house with him every Sabbath day. Had I followed his example and advice, I would have led a different life, and have come to a different end. I was occasionally coming and going to my father's house till I was about sixteen years old, when I left it altogether as a residence. Since I left it I have led a loose and bad life. Drinking and bad company

of all kinds from that time got the better of me, and I went into sins of all kinds. When working amongst all sorts of people at public works, the temptations were very great, and I readily yielded to them. When about nineteen years of age, I was married to my first wife; but this did not mend me. When I wanted any of my children baptised, I was obliged to make my appearance at church for a few days; but I had no other or better object in doing so. My first wife lived about eleven years, and died leaving me with four children. I was a widower about sixteen months and then married my present wife, who has often warned me about my wicked life, and advised me to leave it off and go to church. She is not to blame in any way for my present condition, for had I taken her advice I would never have done anything wrong. No one is to blame but myself. I have been a bad husband and a careless and bad father; I neither showed a good example nor gave proper advice. I sometimes tried to do better, but the wickedness was so into me, that I could not. I often took drink, and used to swear. I was oftener drunk of the Sabbath day that on any other day. Since I got the last child baptised, about three years ago, I was seldom or never at church. I was out of regular work about three months before I committed the crime for which I am about to suffer. My family were rather badly off during that time, but my sister's husband was very kind, and often supplied us with meal. I had, too, sometimes got assistance from John Geddes, and at one time, about two years ago, I got one pound from him, and left my watch as a pledge. After that I sent my daughter to him and got another pound. My family and myself had fever at this time, and were badly off. When I went to him the night before the awful deed was done which made me a murderer, it was with a view to get a little money from him to put over my son's wedding, as I wished to have him married. I arrived at his house about six in the evening, as near as I can judge. To induce him to give me the money, I told him a lie. I said one of the children was dead, and I had no means to bury it. I asked for ten shillings, and at last came to five, but he would not give me it; this was in the morning. We went to bed about ten o'clock, we had no quarrel or angry words that night. As I had said that I wished to bury the child that day, and as I had about twenty miles to walk, I rose about four o'clock in the morning to make him the more readily believe it, and give me the money. He rose at the same time to make me some brose for breakfast, but would not give me any money. We had some angry words, and I insisted to have my watch, but he refused to give me it. I was sitting at the fire, and had the tongs in my hand. He had just put the pot on the fire, and was turning round, when it came into my heart to murder him, and I struck him down with the tongs. He never spoke, but I kept beating him after he was down. I struck him many blows and when he began to stir I took a cord which was lying on the floor, and put it round his neck to strangle him should he come to life again. I then took a purse out of a chest; the purse contained six pounds in silver and two half crowns. I also took a pair of shoes; but I took nothing else. If there was any paper money, I did not see it. I did not take a belt; and being near to death, I solemnly declare that the belt shown in the Court at my trial was my own belt, and that it never was in any one's possession but mine. I lined it, and put the pouch in it myself. I had worn it rather more than five years. I acknowledge that my sentence is just; and I hope my shameful death will be a warning to all who are leading such careless and sinful lives as I have done. This statement and confession has been written at my request, with the view of it being published. It has been read over to me four times, and all is true; and not being able to write, I have put my mark to it, before three witnesses, on this the last day of my life."

25th July 1850

Murder by Poisoning

On this date, William Bennison, a Workman employed by Shotts Iron Company, Leith Walk, Edinburgh, was found guilty at the High Court of Justiciary of the murder of his wife Jean, by mixing some porridge or oatmeal with a quantity of arsenic. Bennison had been married to Jean, his second wife, for about eleven years, however he was additionally tried for bigamy during the proceedings, after enquiries during the murder case found that his first wife, Mary Mullen, although now deceased, had still been alive when he married Jean Hamilton. It was reported that for a long period, the second Mrs Bennison had been in a delicate state of health, caused by an asthmatic complaint. However, on the Friday before she died, she suddenly took very seriously ill with severe pain and vomiting. With the illness continuing over the weekend, Mrs Bennison then died on the Monday morning. At this time, no foul play was suspected, due to her existing medical condition, and she was buried on the Wednesday, with much sympathy being extended to her husband. However, suspicion was raised when two dogs, who had entered the house of the deceased, soon became ill and died, showing signs of poisoning. News of this spread among the neighbours, reaching the deceased's sister, who urged that there should be an investigation. The Sheriff, after some inquiry into the case, granted a warrant for the examination of the body of Mrs Bennison. This examination found a quantity of arsenic present in her stomach, sufficient to have caused her death. Further investigation uncovered that William Bennison had purchased a quantity of arsenic from a druggist's shop in the Kirkgate,

Leith, on the pretence of killing rats. Witnesses confirmed that no rats had been seen in the vicinity of the Bennison's house for around three or four years and no rat holes were found within the house. The druggist also stated that around a time which would coincide with Bennison realising he was under suspicion, Bennison called on him and his wife, requesting them not to mention the purchase of the arsenic. Additionally, it appeared that Bennison refused to seek medical help for his wife before she died, stated as a reason that 'he had no faith in doctors'. Bennison was apprehended and taken to the Calton Jail. Neighbours of Bennison, an Irish immigrant, who was thought to be about thirty two years old, spoke of him being a very religious man, often praying, however there were rumours of him paying undue attention to another female, Margaret Robertson, who also lived in Leith. The trial uncovered that during the previous Spring, there had began to been a cooling in Bennison's attention to his wife and he frequently went out after work, rather than returning home. Witnesses also spoke of seeing him sometimes out walking in the company of Margaret Robertson. The jury after less that twenty minutes, found Bennison guilty of both bigamy and murder. Bennison was said to have shown no emotion at this verdict. The judge, then putting on his black cap, ordained the prisoner to be removed from the bar and detained in the prison and fed on bread and water until Friday, the 16th August 1850, when he should be taken to the place of common execution and hanged.

The day before Bennison's execution, he was taken from the Calton Jail to the Lock up House at the rear of the Advocates' Library at about six o'clock in the morning. Despite the early hour, his emergence at the destination attracted attention, with several people running over to witness the goings on. Bennison, on seeing them, urged his escort to quicken his pace into the building. Once inside he descended the stairs with a vigour which the persons accompanying him found remarkable for a person facing such a fate the next day. Although it was reported that since the trial, Bennison had appeared fairly unaffected by his sentence, eating heartily and sleeping well. For a considerable time on the Thursday, Bennison had the Prison Chaplain and a Clergyman from Leith with him in the Lockup. The erection of the gallows began at eleven o'clock that night and finished between three and four o'clock in the morning. During this time, a crowd of several hundred persons were present, many of whom were described as being from 'the most worthless and depraved portion of the community'. Bailies Law and Fyfe, both Junior Magistrates who were given the duty of seeing the sentence carried out, attended the Sheriff's Room in the County Buildings at half past seven on the morning of Friday 16th August 1850, and made their way to the apartment in the Lock up which Bennison had been moved in preparation for their arrival. The Magistrates were dressed in their official costume, and carried white rods in their hands. On entering the cell, they gave the usual certificate to the Governor of the Jail, who delivered Bennison over to their custody. After a prayer from the Rev. Mr Hay, followed by a hymn, the solemn procession began to walk the distance of two hundred yards to the scaffold. It was said that Bennison's cool and collected appearance never faltered, even when he caught sight of the gallows on entering Liberton's Wynd, and he walked up the steps to the scaffold without appearing to have the slightest trepidation. After five minutes of prayer, the executioner placed the cap over Bennison's head and face and handed him the handkerchief to signal when he was ready. On throwing the handkerchief from him, Bennison said aloud "The Lord Jesus have mercy on my soul". The drop then fell, and after struggling for a few moments with great violence, thought to be due to the rope not being properly adjusted, all signs of life ceased. The body, after hanging for about an hour, was cut down and placed in a coffin, to be buried in the course of the afternoon within the grounds of the Calton Jail. The crowd had been immense, extending as far up the Lawnmarket as the corner of the West Bow, and as for down the High Street as the Police Office. All windows which had a view of the scaffold also being filled with spectators. This crowd, it was estimated, amounted to twenty thousand persons. As this had been the first execution in Edinburgh since James Bryce in 1844, upwards of two hundred and fifty police were present on this day, however there was no disorder in the crowd, who seemed to show very little emotion. It was reported that Bennison had written a confession a week or two before the execution, however on this occasion it had not been handed over to the press for publication.

The following month it was reported in the newspapers that important facts relating to the death of Bennison's first wife, had been ascertained. It appeared that Bennison had accompanied his first wife, Mary Mullen from Ireland to Airdrie, where they remained in lodgings for a week. At this time, Mary seemed to be in good health, with only a slight complaint of feeling sea sick on the voyage. However, she then for two days suffered incessant vomiting, which was accompanied by an excessive thirst. As with his second wife, no doctor was called for, with Bennison this time giving the reason that he could not afford it. Mary's death surprised the other lodgers within the house and seemed to at the time have aroused suspicion. However she was buried the next day, with Bennison leaving town the day after the funeral.

17th April 1864

The Tragedy at Ratho

On Saturday, 17th April 1864, a young woman named Jane Seton, described as 'a highly respectable young woman', employed as a nurse with Mr Robert Tod, was murdered by George Bryce, a Carter. George Bryce, who was the nephew of the executed James Bryce, was employed by his father, who had a small farm and kept a public house in Ratho. It would appear that Bryce had been frequenting Mr Tod's house in order to visit the cook, with whom he wished to have a relationship. However due to him being of 'dissipated and degraded habits', the nurse, Jane Seton made it clear that she did not approve of him and persuaded the cook to break all contact with him. Knowing of Jane Seton's interference, Bryce took a great dislike to her and was reported to have frequently expressed his determination to have his revenge. On the morning of the 17th, Bryce left his father's house and proceeded to the Tod household. On arriving there, he asked the cook whether Jane Seton was in the house, to which she replied that she was, but told him not to enter. Bryce pushed her aside, and made his way to the nursery, where he pushed Seton to the floor and attempted to strangle her. Mrs Tod, hearing the nurse's screams, rushed to the nursery, grabbed an umbrella, and dealt Bryce a number of blows to the hands, forcing him to release his grip. Seton fled the house, followed by Bryce, and made her way to the house of Mr Binnie, the Joiner. On her arrival there, Bryce had caught up with her and taking a razor from his pocket, cut her throat from ear to ear. Bryce rushed from the scene of the murder, but the incident had been witnessed by Mrs Tod, who had followed him across the valley. He was apprehended an hour later by Constable Mills of the County Police, and two quarrymen who had assisted in the search. An attempt was made by Bryce, to cut his own throat when he realised he was cornered, however he was prevented from this and only managed to cause a slight wound on the left side of his neck. Bryce denied any recollection of the circumstances that had occurred that morning and was conveyed to the Calton Jail later in the day. At his trial, the theory given by the defence was that he was insane at the time the murder was committed. The judge advised the jury that they must decide whether it was likely that a person, who had always been treated as a sane person, however peculiar he may have been in his temper and disposition, could suddenly become insane to the effect of becoming irresponsible for the consequences of his acts. The jury, after three quarters of an hour, returned to Court with a unanimous verdict of guilty, but recommended mercy for Bryce, due to the 'low organisation of his mental faculties'. The Lord Justice General stating that their recommendation would be forwarded to the proper quarter, pronounced the sentence of death, to be carried out on the morning of the 21st June 1864.

On the Saturday prior to the execution, Bryce's mother, father, three brothers and two sisters paid him a farewell visit in his prison cell. The parting was reported to have been a painful experience, particularly for the parents, during which Bryce seemed to realise the agony by which his crime had affected his family. On the Sunday, Bryce attended a service conducted by the Chaplain, after which the Chaplain remained with him for some time. On the Monday, Bryce was removed from the Jail to the Courts' Buildings in Parliament Square, in preparation for the execution the next morning. This execution took place in front of an immense crowd of spectators, consisting of what was described as 'every species of ruffianism, wretchedness and vagabondism'. However, in the short time prior to the hour of execution, the behaviour of the mob seemed to calm and a deep sense of horror seemed to arise from the crowd when Bryce appeared on the scaffold.

7th October 1865

Dreadful Tragedy in Edinburgh – Murder by a Maniac of his Mother and Sister

In Dalrymple Crescent, Grange, Edinburgh, a 'dreadful tragedy was enacted'. John Hunter, a man aged 30, who is described as being 'weakly in body and erratic in his disposition' and having 'a slightly imbecile appearance' had within the last few days prior to the incident been exhibiting some signs of restlessness and on this occasion had been interrupted by his mother and sister whilst trying to leave the house. Irritated by their interference, he is said to have murdered them with an iron rod. Hunter's mental state was said to have been such that for the last six years, his friends and relatives had kept him in close confinement within his parents' house. Hunter had been seen by a neighbour immediately before the incident, making his way to the street, with his mother and sister following him and attempting to stop him. Outside the gate, his mother put her hand on his shoulder, to which he turned around and knocked her down with the iron rod, then struck his sister with it. Their deaths were thought to have been instantaneous. It was reported that Hunter was sad, depressed and studious, and having mania that assumed a religious form, where he thought of himself as an important Scriptural person. It was stated that he had been treated with considerable kindness by his family. After the murder he apparently ran into the back garden and hid in the greenhouse, concealing the iron bar under his coat. The alarm spread rapidly and a large number of neighbours and workmen in the neighbourhood were soon on the spot, and the police called for. Hunter finally came out of the greenhouse when the police and his father and brother arrived. It was said that he appeared to show no grief for the death of his mother and sister and refused to answer any questions put to him, although he accompanied the officers to the police station without resistance. He was examined in the presence of the Sheriff, where he made no comment, was formally committed and conveyed to Calton Jail. This double murder excited great interest in the usually quiet neighbourhood in which it occurred and people began to come from considerable distances to witness the scene of the murder, to the extent that extra police were put at the scene to stop people from trying to obtain blood marked mementoes from the pavement.

31st May 1878

Execution of Eugene Chantrelle

At eight o'clock on this date, in the prison of Edinburgh, the sentence of death was carried out on Eugene Chantrelle for the poisoning of his wife. Chantrelle was widely known in the city as an accomplished teacher. Public opinion seemed to be that a verdict of not proven should have been found in this case and efforts were made to obtain a remission of the capital sentence, however Chantrelle was quite clear that he would rather die than have life long imprisonment. By this point in the Victorian era, executions were all conducted within prisons, with the spectacle of the public execution having been banned in 1868. This was therefore the first execution to take place within a prison, and a large crowd gathered on Calton Hill long before the event was to take place. Precautions had been taken however, to prevent the public from being able to witness any of the proceedings by the erection of a screen at the front entrance of the jail, to cut off a view they would have otherwise had of the procession making its way to the place of execution. All that was seen therefore from Calton Hill, was the hoisting of the black flag in due time.

31st March 1884

Double Execution in Edinburgh

Robert Flockhart Vickers and William Innes suffered the extreme penalty of the law on this date, for the murder of two Gamekeepers the previous December. The execution took place in private, within the Calton Prison, with only officials, three clergymen and representatives of five newspapers permitted to be present. As is usually the case, the two men spent most of the few days prior to their execution with the Chaplain, engaging in prayer. It was reported that they both slept well on the night before the execution and rose at 5 o'clock in the morning, when they had breakfast. After breakfast, Vickers had an interview with the Rev. Mr Wilson, with whom he engaged in conversation for a considerable time. He entrusted Mr Wilson with several messages of love to his wife and children and stated that he hoped that the event which was soon to take place would be 'rest for him'. He also stated that he deplored the bad example he had shown his children, and the evil effect which his conduct might entail upon them. Vickers also requested that Mr Wilson call on the families of the murdered gamekeepers to express his sorrow at the trouble he had brought upon them and to let them know that he died praying for them. Innes had requested that the Rev. Mr Keay stay with him until the hour of his execution. Although the public could no longer witness executions, they would still gather outside the prison and wait until the black flag was hoisted, announcing to all that the hanging had taken place. On this day, a large crowd, numbering about 5000, mostly consisting of men and boys, but with a few females included, congregated on Calton Hill, as near as possible to the only point in which a glimpse could be obtained of a portion of the roof of the wooden shed within which the execution was to take place. It was said that many of the people present were from the mining community and some of them had been acquainted with the condemned men. It would appear that on this occasion there was no demonstration of feeling, and silence prevailed among the crowd. Some time after seven o'clock, Baillies Roberts and Clark, the Magistrates deputed to see the death warrant carried out, accompanied by three of the city officers, were admitted within the prison gate. Also in attendance were the Clerk to the Magistrates, the Prison Surgeon, the Chief Constable of Edinburgh, the Governor of the prison, and other officials. At 25 minutes to eight, the Magistrates, having donned their robes of office, proceeded to a building at the south eastern extremity of the prison. On the first floor of the building, there was a small chamber within the Surgeon's room, where preparations had been made for holding a brief service. The prisoners, having met on the landing outside, which was the first time they had seen each other since their trial, greeted each other warmly, then entered the room for the service. After prayers, the executioner, James Berry, entered the room, accompanied by his assistant, Richard Chester. The two prisoners shook hands with the assembled group in the chamber and also with the executioners. The Magistrates and others then left and proceeded to the place of execution. For the condemned men, a door from the corridor opened upon the platform of the scaffold. Two paces forward from the door, hung the fatal cords with nooses ready, hung from a large cross beam. Vickers and Innes, without weakness, walked to the scaffold, the executioners quickly drawing the white caps over their heads. On his cap being adjusted however, Vickers said loudly "Lord have mercy on me a sinner!". Innes then repeated this line. With the nooses carefully adjusted, and the medical officers having examined them and found them to be properly placed, the signal was given, and as the bolt fell, the two men were hanged. It was said that death appeared to be instantaneous.

The crime for which these men had been hanged, was detailed as follows: The two men, both 37 years old, whose wives and families lived in Gorebridge, were Miners, who were also prone to the activity of 'poaching'. On the night of Friday, the 14th December 1883, the two men set off on a poaching expedition armed with double barrelled guns. As the night was clear, and although cold, favourable weather for poaching purposes, James Grosset, the Head Gamekeeper on the estate of Rosebery, together with John Fortune, another gamekeeper, and John McDiarmid, a rabbit trapper, all went out to watch for trespassers. After several hours, having spotted no trespassers, the three men parted shortly before three o'clock in the morning and made their separate ways homeward. However, Grosset had no sooner entered his house when he heard a shot fired. He called on his two other companions and armed only with their sticks, and no other weapons, went in search of the persons who had fired the shot. On hearing a second shot, they were guided towards Westerpark of Redside, near the bridge over the Edgelaw

Reservoir. When they reached a field there, they kept undercover of a fence and moved along until Vickers and Innes came into view. Having failed to see the gamekeepers, the two men entered the field, and once aware of the presence of the gamekeepers, Vickers and Innes started retreating backwards up the hill. Grosset, recognising Innes, called out to him that there was no point running away as he knew who he was. At that point, both Innes and Vickers pointed their guns and fired. McDiarmid fell first, shot by Vickers, and Fortune fell from a shot fired by Innes. Innes also fired at Grosset, who was hit in the back by four pellets. Realising he had not killed Grosset, Innes fired again, but the shot missed and Grosset was able to run for assistance while Vickers and Innes had to stop and reload their guns. The two men were apprehended the next day.

18th February 1889

The Edinburgh Baby Murderer

A young woman named Jessie King was placed at the bar at the High Court of Justiciary on this date, charged with the murder of three children. The details of the charges were that: in April or May 1888, in a house in Ann's Court, Canonmills, Edinburgh, at that time occupied by Thomas Pearson, Jessie King murdered Alex Gunn, aged twelve months by strangling him; in September 1888, in a house in Cheyne Street, Stockbridge, Edinburgh, occupied by Thomas Pearson, Jessie King murdered Violet Duncan Tomlinson, aged six weeks old by strangling or suffocating her; also in October or November 1887, in a house in Dalkeith Road, Edinburgh, occupied by Thomas Pearson, Jessie King murdered Walter Anderson Campbell, aged five months, by strangling him. There was a large attendance of the public in the court that day, and King, who was 27 years old and originally from Glasgow, admitted the first two charges, but pleaded not guilty to the third charge. King's original statement was read out to the court, in which she stated that she had adopted the child Gunn, and that her partner Thomas Pearson who at first was unwilling to take the child in, changed his mind when she told him that she had received £3 from the mother, at which time he agreed that the baby could stay for three or four weeks. King said that they kept him from April until the end of May 1888, however when she then found she was unable to support the child, she attempted to get him admitted to a destitute home, however this was refused on the grounds that the child was illegitimate. King stated that after this she had become very much the worse of drink and strangled the child, as she had no means to support it. When the child was dead, she placed the body in a locked box, and kept it there until the next day, when she took it out and put it in a cupboard, where it remained for three days, after which the couple moved from Canonmills to Stockbridge. At this point, the body was placed in a cellar in the Stockbridge house, later being removed from there at the beginning of October and placed on a piece of vacant ground at Cheyne Street. King stated that Pearson had known nothing of this death, as she had told him she had managed to get the child admitted to a home. On the matter of the child Tomlinson, King said that this child had also been adopted by her, and this time she was paid the sum of £2 for the baby. King maintained that Pearson had known nothing about this at the time, and on getting the child home, she gave her some whisky to keep it quiet. However, it would seem that the whisky was stronger that she thought and the child started to choke. King responded by placing her hand on the child's mouth, killing her. This body was also placed in the cellar, where it remained until it was discovered by the police. On the third charge, the murder of Walter Campbell, many witnesses were called, with one witness, Janet Anderson, explaining that in May 1887, her sister Elizabeth Campbell, had died and King had offered to adopt the child if the father would pay a fee. The father, David Finlay, gave evidence that he had handed the child to King and Pearson and paid them £5. He stated that they told him their surname was Stewart. A neighbour from Dalkeith Road, where they were living at this time, gave evidence that they arrived home suddenly with a child at that time, however three months later the child disappeared, and when she asked King what had happened, King told her she had taken him home as he was ill. Shortly afterwards, King and Pearson left the locality. It seems that the house in Dalkeith Road was thoroughly searched and no remains of a child were found. The third charge was eventually disregarded and the jury found King guilty of the first two charges. The judge, putting on his black cap, sentenced Jessie King to be hanged within the Calton Jail on the 11th March. Whilst being sentenced, King gradually subsided into a hysterical fit and had to be carried downstairs to the cells.

As Jessie King was thought to be a 'woman of very low intelligence', there was some public opinion that she had been tempted by others due to living in poverty and that she was bearing the blame for the wickedness of the others who gave their children into her keeping. King had also later stated that she had been induced to confess in her statement, being advised that if she did so, she would get off with a fairly brief prison sentence. A petition was signed by 2000 persons asking for a reprieve for King, however this proved unsuccessful.

The scaffold for the execution was erected close to a corridor between the male and female sections of the prison. Berry, the executioner had arrived in Edinburgh a few days previous to complete his preparations. King, a Roman Catholic, had been attended by a priest the night before the execution was to take place. On the morning of Friday 11th March 1889, at eight o'clock, Jessie King was hanged, death was said to be instantaneous. A crowd of around 2000 people had gathered outside on the Calton Hill to see the black flag raised.

Hangmen

At the time of James Bryce's execution in 1844, the hangman of Edinburgh was John Scott, who was previously the hangman of Aberdeen. However, it would seem that the execution of James Bryce was carried out by John Murdoch, the hangman of Glasgow. It is not clear why this was the case, however, the execution of Bryce was the first one that had been carried out in four years, with the last one, the execution of a man named Wemyss, taking place in 1840. John Scott had been the hangman at Wemyss' execution and had caused quite a scene by drawing the wrong bolt and in his desperation to complete the task, began stamping on the machinery in an attempt to put it in motion. In the end an official who was present, had to come up the stairs of the scaffold and draw the correct bolt. As described in the previous chapter, John Scott died in 1847, murdered by James Edey. After his death, it was felt that there was no need to appoint another executioner in Edinburgh, as so few executions took place there. Therefore, when an executioner was needed, they were brought in from another part of the country. James Berry of Bradford was once such executioner, who was brought in to carry out the execution of Robert Flockhart and William Innes in 1884. Berry worked as an executioner from 1884 – 1892, after which he gave public lectures on hanging.

Chapter 5

Forensic Medicine and the Victorian Expert Witness

Dissecting Room, Edinburgh 1889

In Victorian Edinburgh, there was a growing importance in Medical Jurisprudence, the branch of study which connected medicine and law which aimed to prepare medical students for providing good evidence, and for law students to learn good forensic knowledge. The first Professorship of Forensic Medicine to be established in a British University occurred in Edinburgh in 1801, and during the 19th century there were many advances in the discovery of physiological action of drugs and poisons, and in anatomy, physiology and microscopy. Often, in the more complex cases involving murder or culpable homicide, expert witnesses could be called to give evidence. These expert witnesses were often prominent medical practitioners of the time, such as Dr Joseph Bell, who taught Arthur Conan Doyle when he began his studies at Edinburgh University in 1877 and is thought to be the inspiration behind the Sherlock Holmes character, due to the skills in observation and deduction he applied to his medical work. Bell, a lecturer at Edinburgh University Medical School in the 19th century, in his teaching emphasised the importance of close observation in making a diagnosis. He was considered a pioneer in Forensic Science. Conan Doyle, whilst working as Bell's Clerk, had to take patient notes prior to Bell examining the patient and he would often be astounded as Bell deduced all sorts of information without having to ask either Conan Doyle or the patient a question. Henry Duncan Littlejohn, lecturer in Medical Jurisprudence at Edinburgh University, was also called upon to give his medical opinion in criminal cases. Littlejohn was also appointed as Edinburgh's Medical Officer of Health in 1862, whilst also continuing his duties of 'Surgeon of Police'. Littlejohn appeared in many important trials in the latter part of the Victorian era, and was appointed Chair of Forensic Medicine in 1897. In his opening lecture in this post, Littlejohn spoke of the large amount of work still to be done with regard to the development of forensic medicine, pointing out that whilst all the existing departments of medical study were already provided with a practical department, forensic medicine, at that time, was merely taught in a theoretical matter'. Speaking of its connection with crime, Littlejohn also pointed out the difference existing between any ordinary case of illness and one in which the commission of a great crime was connected. He had found in practice that the investigation of a criminal case in a practical manner lent an interest to the subject matter of his lectures, which enabled the student to enter enthusiastically into fuller discussions, therefore making him a more satisfactory witness when called upon to give evidence in a Court of law. Another expert witness often used was Dr Patrick Heron Watson, a friend of Joseph Bell, who it has been suggested, may have been the inspiration for Conan Doyle's 'Dr Watson' character, as he had a very similar background to that of Conan Doyle's Watson.

Edinburgh University © Peter Stubbs, Edinphoto

These men were often called upon to perform postmortems when a death was thought to be caused by a criminal act. Forensic Medicine was very much in its infancy and science was not widely used in criminal investigations, however more and more emphasis was being placed on medical evidence in trials.

The Leven Wife Murder

Dr Joseph Bell appeared as an expert witness in the case of Robert Bowman in 1875, who was accused of murdering his wife Isabella by stabbing her. Bowman, who was said to have previously displayed 'malice and illwill' against his wife, pleaded not guilty, on the grounds of insanity. An engine driver named George Kilgour and a fireman, Peter Haldane had been present in Bowman's house on the Saturday night prior to the incident. Kilgour stated that Bowman and his wife had both been affected by drink, however during the time he was there they appeared to be on friendly terms. He went on to say that he had known Bowman when he was station agent at Muiredge and always understood him to be a heavy drinker, who had a strange look and conducted the business at Muiredge in a loose manner. Peter Haldane gave a similar impression of Bowman. Janet Walker, who lived opposite the Bowman's, gave evidence that at 7 a.m. on the Sunday, she heard Mrs Bowman swearing at her husband and shortly afterwards Mrs bowman came to Mrs Walker's door in her night dress and asked her to go across to her husband and 'reprimand him for his treatment of her'. On entering the Bowman's house, she found Robert Bowman seated by the fire in his working clothes. Mrs Walker told the court that both of the Bowmans' seemed to be much affected by drink and that Robert Bowman told her he was going to church. An hour or so later, Mrs Walker received the same request again from Mrs Bowman, who this time stated that her husband had 'begun to rage'. Mrs Walker did not go to the house this time and told the court that shortly after that she heard a scream coming from the house, but thought nothing of it. It seemed that such occurrences were not unusual in the Bowmans' house, with Mrs Walker giving evidence that Bowman had previously used violence towards his wife. The next day Mrs Bowman's father and sister came round and Mrs Walker went in to the Bowmans' house with them, where they found the dead body of Mrs Bowman in the bed, covered over with the bed clothes. Robert's brother, Archibald Bowman told the court that his brother had came to his father's house on the day of the incident and had attended church with the family, without his wife, who usually accompanied him. On the day that Mrs Bowman's body was found, Archibald Bowman found that his brother had gone to his father's house and remained there until 10 p.m., when he was apprehended. The body was initially examined by two local doctors, who found an incised wound, 1 ¾ inches in length, and 3 inches in depth, penetrating the chest. The doctors were of the opinion that this wound had caused her death and that the deceased could not have been in the position in which she was found when the wound was inflicted. Bowman told the court that his wife was addicted to drinking, and that he had been betrayed into marrying her. He also said that he hated her for this and that she was constantly irritating and annoying him. As to the question of his sanity, evidence was given that Bowman was somewhat below the average intellect and that his mind was 'not of a high order, but what he had of it was sound'. Dr Watson, senior surgeon to the Royal Infirmary, Edinburgh, said that it was quite possible that the wound could be caused by a 'stout woman like the deceased falling on the knife'. Dr Watson advised that he had, with the assistance of his resident surgeon and class assistant, conducted this experiment upon a dead body and found that a very similar wound was produced. Dr Joseph Bell, lecturer on surgery, Edinburgh, said that he thought it was extremely improbable from the direction of the wound, that the prisoner could have inflicted it and that it was more probable that it was caused by Mrs Bowman falling on the knife. However, after an adjournment Bowman changed his plea to 'guilty' of the crime of Culpable Homicide and was sentenced to fifteen years penal servitude.

A Charge of Culpable Homicide

Two young men, named John Wood and William Smeatton were charged in 1878 with the Culpable Homicide of John Boyd, a Mason, residing at Craiglockhart Cottages, Colinton. At the trial, it was established that the deceased had spent the evening in Pirie's public house in William Street and had left along with the two accused. George Stewart, leaving the public house about fifteen minutes after the three men, saw a crowd opposite no. 30 William Street and on closer inspection he saw Boyd lying at the foot of the stair, with a pool of blood around him. Wood and Smeatton, who were standing beside Boyd, told Stewart that Boyd had fallen down the stairs. Neither Wood, Smeatton or Stewart gave any assistance to Boyd. Another witness, John Alexander gave evidence that he had seen the two accused running after Boyd, and then Wood striking him on the chest. Alexander stated that Boyd then ran into the entry at no. 30 William Street, followed by Wood and Smeatton, after which he heard Smeatton shout "give him one", and immediately afterwards Alexander heard a heavy fall. The post mortem examination carried out by Dr Joseph Bell and Dr Littlejohn, found that death had resulted from fracture of the skull and rupture of the brain, caused by external violence, the injuries being such as would have been caused by a fall down the stairs. The jury, after an absence of five minutes, returned a verdict of guilty, with Wood and Smeatton being sentenced to three months imprisonment each.

Attack with a Hatchet

In January 1893, a case went to trial involving a man named Patrick Griffin, who was charged with having killed Edward Wynn with a hatchet and a poker, in the house of labourer, Martin Moffat in the Lawnmarket. Moffat gave evidence that Griffin came to the house on the day of the incident and had been told to leave as his company was not wanted. However, Griffin came back in shortly afterwards, seized a hatchet which was lying by the side of the fire, struck Moffat with it, and when Wynn tried to take it from him, Griffin struck him on the head. As Wynn was being escorted downstairs, Griffin struck him with a poker. The post mortem examination had been carried out by Dr Littlejohn and Dr Joseph Bell, who found a wound on the scalp about one inch in length on the left side of the head. The bones of the nose were fractured and there was a wound on the back of his right hand. Their opinion, as a result of the examination, was that Wynn died from acute inflammation of the membranes of the brain, caused by external violence. Dr Littlejohn, giving evidence, stated that judging from the peculiar indentation of the bone of the skull, some weapon must have been used, and that the hatchet shown was a likely instrument to have produced the indentation. Dr Littlejohn also said that in his opinion, if the wound had been attended to immediately after the injury was inflicted; it was highly probable that he would have recovered. This was corroborated by Dr Bell. Other witnesses interviewed said that Griffin had been chased downstairs by three men, who were somewhat the worse for drink and that Griffin had taken refuge in a neighbouring house, but was set upon by three men in the close upon leaving this house. The jury however, found Griffin guilty of Culpable Homicide and he was sentenced to six months imprisonment.

Chapter 6

Prison

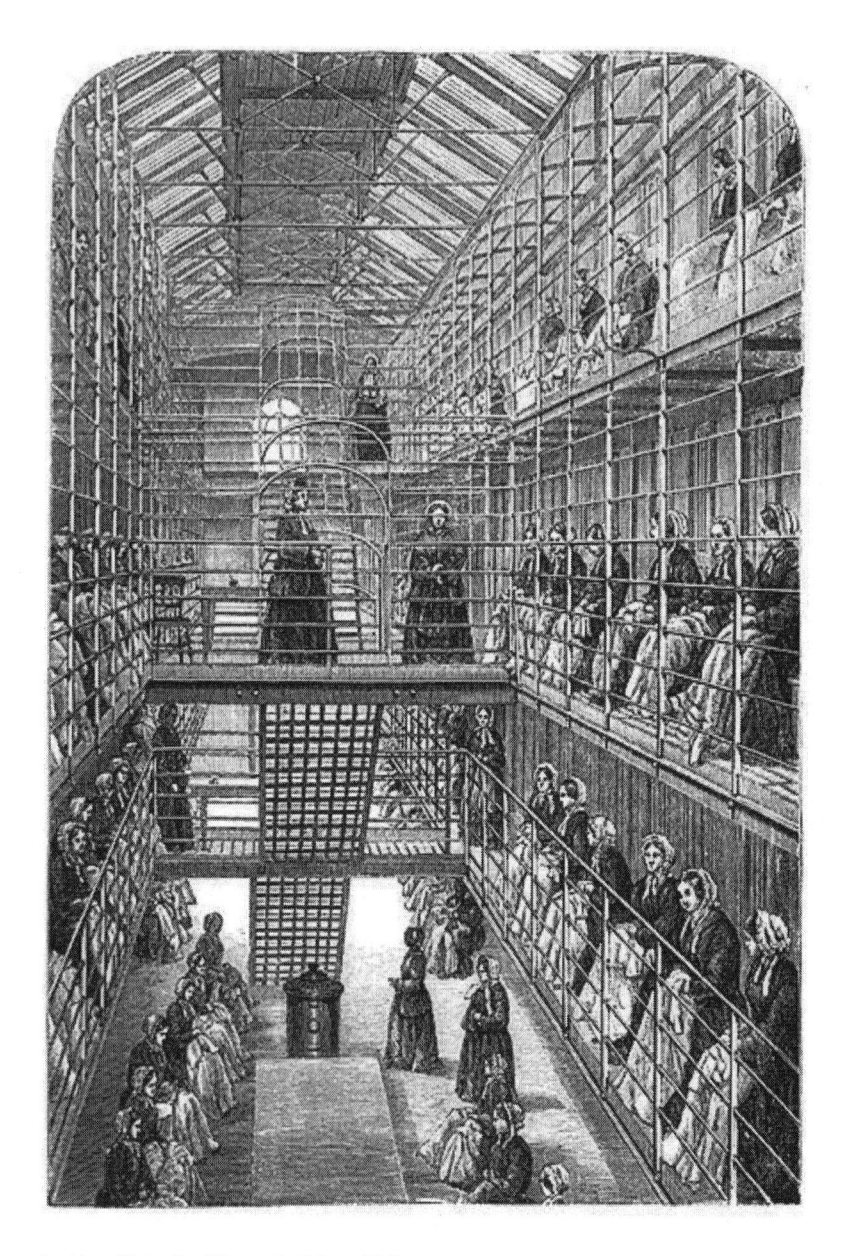

Inside a Victorian Women's Prison 1862

Calton Jail

Calton Jail (c) Peter Stubbs, Edinburgh

Calton Jail in Edinburgh opened in 1817, replacing the old Tolbooth, which was said to be obstructing the Royal Mile. This jail held male and female prisoners, in separate wings. As we have heard, this jail was also the setting for executions after public hangings stopped in 1868. It is said that at least eight murderers are buried in unmarked graves on Calton Hill, which would originally have been within the prison grounds. Calton jail remained in use until 1926, replaced by Saughton Prison on the outskirts of the city. St Andrew's House now stands on the site of the old Calton jail, however parts of the old wall and the Governor's house can still be seen.

This jail and accompanying bridewell started out as two separate institutions, however they were merged into one in 1841, becoming known as he prison of Edinburgh. Although an improvement on the old Tolbooth, Calton jail had many problems of its own. An article appeared in the Scotsman on 23rd August 1837, regarding 'Irregularities in the Jail' gives us a picture of the prison conditions at the start of Victoria's reign:

'The Magistrates and Jail Committee gave in their report on certain irregularities which were said to have taken place in the Jail.... Case of John Finlayson – This individual was imprisoned upon the 31st day of March, having been found guilty of theft in the Police Court, and sentenced to twenty days' confinement. He was a very dissipated character, and had been much addicted to drinking, and had no fixed dwelling place. It appears that at the time he was admitted, the jail was in a very crowded state, although not more so that it had been for several weeks previously, and he and another two men were put into the same cell, and slept in the same bed. On the first and second mornings the two persons who slept with him complained to the turnkey that Finlayson was of such dirty habits that they could not sleep with him; and finding that this was true, he admonished him that if a repetition of the occurrence complained of took place; he would be under the necessity of reporting him to the governor. The nuisance continuing, he was, upon the fourth night, in consequence of the governor's orders, removed to a dark cell, being the only one in the jail at the time where he could sleep alone.... It appears that shortly before Finlayson was so removed, the blankets had been taken out of the dark cell, and there can be no doubt that for three; if not four nights, Finlayson was allowed to lie in that cell without blankets, and at that time the weather was unusually cold. It also appears that, although Finlayson's dirty habits were the result of

paralysis, it does not seem that the doctor was informed of his infirm condition until the 15th of April.'

Realising the problems with this jail and many others at the time, on the 28th March 1838, an 'Abstract of a Bill to Improve Prisons and Prison Discipline in Scotland' was drafted, which appeared in the Scotsman. This Bill recommended that:

'Provision should be made for the erection and maintenance of more secure and convenient prisons, and for the better management thereof... and the appointment of a Board of Directors of Prisons...with power to erect and maintain proper prisons, and to regulate the discipline and management of all prisons in Scotland.'

In response to this, the Scotsman featured the following comment:

'Had the plan been earlier adopted, of bringing periodically before the public, the whole facts connected with our jails, their filth, their disorderly condition, their tendency to generate crime and propagate disease, the Government would have been shamed out of its apathy, and compelled to adopt efficient measures of reform many years ago.'

However, a report on the 'State of Crime in the County of Midlothian' in the Scotsman on 14th August 1839, doesn't show any great changes. The report stated that the prisons of Edinburgh had been unusually full during part of the year, and detailed the conditions within the Calton Jail:

'During the last year a new kitchen and washhouse have been built, most of the day rooms have been enlarged, and part of the accommodation

hitherto reserved for debtors has been cut off and added to that of the criminals. Within the last six months, also work to some extent has been introduced for some of the male criminals; but in other respects the jail remains in much the same state as at the time of my last visit. At the time I made various recommendations for its improvement, but few of them have been carried into operation...With rare exceptions the prisoners were quite idle. They chiefly occupied their time in gambling, obscene language, singing bawdy songs, recounting their adventures, smoking, quarrelling and fighting.'

The author of the report, Frederic Hill, the Inspector of Prisons, had also spoken to prisoners in the Bridewell part of the jail, with most of them stating that 'drink, women, gaming or idle company' were to blame for their offending, with by far the most common of these causes being drink. Other prisoners spoken to were habitual thieves, one of whom advised that:

'Stealing is a matter of regular business. Most of the thieves know each other, and know the circumstances of the various robberies that are committed. They associate much together. The chief body of the thieves in Edinburgh live in the wynds and closes out of High Street.'

Another report by Frederick Hill in 1841, highlighted the problems with the number of debtors being sent to prison, which seemed to be taking up much of the time and attention of the governor and pointed out that "the room which they occupy, which is much greater than that of an equal number of criminal prisoners, can be ill spared in the present crowded state of the prison". Another concern at the time, was of the number of women sent to prison for prostitution, stating that "of the 240 female prisoners lately in confinement, the governor believes that 200 were prostitutes. The governor attributes the great number of this class of prisoners in part to the difficulty which females have in getting employment in Edinburgh, owing to the want of manufactures. He states that if a servant once loses her situation with an injured character she has scarcely any other resource than prostitution".

Juvenile Offenders

There were growing concerns during Victoria's reign as to the number of children serving prison sentences. Captain Kincaid, an Inspector of Prisons highlighted this in 1849 in his report on Scottish Prisons, in which he spoke of the 'defective state of the laws of Scotland in their provisions for the punishment of juvenile offences'. Captain Kincaid expressed concern over several cases he had become aware of where children had been committed to prison for very trivial acts, such as one child who served 14 days for stealing apples. He also noted that on their first arrival at a prison, children were full of tears and dread, however within a few days this fear was removed and they ended up of the opinion that prison was not as bad a place as they had expected, and therefore usually receiving another prison sentence for some other crime shortly afterwards. It was recognised at the time that juvenile offenders were often neglected children with no one to protect or care for them and Kincaid thought that a better system would be to place these children in a reformatory school in order to educate them and provide them with trades, skills and discipline so that they might go on to lead a more productive life, with the cost of providing these schools being more cost effective in the long run if the children could be reformed, instead of becoming habitual criminals and having to be maintained by the public for life. Kincaid also observed that more had to be done in communities, to make 'worthless parents do their duty'. This idea of reformatory schools was a popular one and in 1850, following the report of a Parliamentary Committee on Criminal and Destitute Children, a Bill was introduced 'for the better care and reformation of juvenile offenders', by establishing reformatory schools for young people, under sixteen years of age, convicted of offences under Summary Procedure. Several difficulties were however pointed out which delayed schools of this type opening, such as the religious difficulty which might be experienced. As they would be providing an education, which would include a religious education, the question was raised as to whether there should be 'catholic reformatories' and 'protestant reformatories'. Another point made within an article in the Scotsman in 1858, was that all discussion so far on the subject had referred to the juvenile offenders as 'boys', however it would be inevitable that provisions would have to be made for girls who offended. The same article also pointed out that reformatories should compliment the existing 'ragged or industrial school'. Ragged schools were schools provided for destitute children in order that they should receive some sort of education. Industrial schools were used for children whose behavior had become a cause for concern, but who had not yet committed a crime. The purpose of the industrial school was not only to provide children with an education, but also to teach them trades which they might use to gain employment in later life. There was much debate as to whether the cost of maintaining children in the reformatories should be recovered from the parents and whether this system was likely to be workable.

However, despite the perceived difficulties, by 1862 the Girls House of Refuge and the Wellington Farm School were both in operation as reformatory schools. The Girls House of Refuge focused on receiving daily scripture; lessons in reading, writing and arithmetic; and additionally sewing, knitting and training for various useful types of employment. The Wellington Farm School focused mainly on outdoor agricultural work and also skills such as carpentry, tailoring and shoemaking, along with education similar to the girls' school. An annual meeting a year after the opening of the boys' school reported that 'the conduct of the boys as inmates of the school had been such as to give the greatest encouragement to expect a favourable result when they are sent out to the various occupations for which they have been trained'.

Overall, many Victorians thought the reformatories were a good thing for children at risk of leading a life of crime by, in the words of Judge Colston in 1896, 'preventing their ever coming into contact with crime or immorality while they were resident there'. A report published in 1898, again highlighted 'lack of parental care and the evil environment of childhood' as the main causes of the criminal career.

Acknowledgements

I would like to thank the following organisations for their assistance:

The National Library of Scotland
The Scotsman
The Glasgow Herald
The National Archives of Scotland

Additional thanks to Peter Stubbs of Edinphoto for the use of all the engravings which have been used as illustrations and also for the use of the following drawings and photographs:

Advocates Close
Princes Street Looking East

All other images are from the author's own collection.

Bibliography

The Law Society of Scotland 'A General History of Scots Law (19th Century)

James Douglas-Hamilton (ed.),The Sheriff Court Districts (Alteration of Boundaries) Order 1996, Office of Public Sector Information, March 29, 1996

Livingston, Sheila, Confess and be Hanged

Bland, James, The Common Hangman

Maitland, Justice and Police

Information has also been sourced online from the following organisations and websites:

The National Archives of Scotland

The Scottish Government

Victorian Crime and Punishment

www.police-information.co.uk

Edinphoto

Archiveshub.ac.uk

Scottish Court Service

Scottish Law Online

Glossary

Area sneak – a person who lurks around dwelling houses for the purposes of stealing

Blackguard – a scoundrel

Bridewell – a House of Correction

Delerium Tremens – an altered mental state caused by alcohol withdrawal

Drag – horse drawn vehicle

Fast day – a religious holiday

Industrial School – a school to help children who were destitute, who had not committed any serious crime but were at risk of becoming criminals

Journeyman – a trader or crafter who has completed an apprenticeship

Landed proprietor – a landowner, or owner of an estate

Laudanum - a wildly popular drug during the Victorian era. It was an opium-based painkiller prescribed for everything from headaches to tuberculosis. As it was cheaper than gin, it was often used as a recreational drug

Muriatic acid – Now known as Hydrochloric acid, it is a solution of hydrogen chloride in water that is highly corrosive

Not Proven verdict - an acquittal used when the judge or jury does not have enough evidence to convict but is not sufficiently convinced of the defendant's innocence to bring in a "not guilty" verdict

Omnibus – a horse drawn bus used for public transport

Overman - a person who supervises others

Porter - a dark-coloured style of beer

Reformatory – a school for juvenile offenders who had committed more serious crimes

Reset - feloniously receiving or retaining goods, obtained by theft, robbery etc., knowing that they have been dishonestly appropriated

Transportation - the deporting of convicted criminals to a penal colony

Uttering - knowingly circulating counterfeit money with intent to defraud

Victualling store – a store containing food provisions

Victorian Money Conversion Guide

As a guide, the following amounts in Victorian money are roughly equivalent to our money today:

1870	*2016*
£1	£45.70
1s	£2.29
1d	£0.19

£ = Pounds Sterling

s = Shillings

d = Pence

Source: The National Archives

Printed in Great Britain
by Amazon